SKILLS IN

RELIGIOUS

STUDIES

Book 3

FOUNDATION EDITION

S C MERCIER

Heinemann Educational Publishers
Halley Court, Jordan Hill, Oxford, OX2 8EJ
a division of Reed Educational & Professional Publishing Ltd

OXFORD MELBOURNE AUCKLAND
JOHANNESBURG BLANTYRE GABORONE
IBADAN PORTSMOUTH NH(USA) CHICAGO

Text © S C Mercier, 2001

First published in 2001

British Library Cataloguing in Publication Data
A catalogue record for this book is available from the British Library

ISBN 0 435 302094
05 04 03 02 01
9 8 7 6 5 4 3 2 1

Designed by Ken Vail Graphic Design, Cambridge
Picture research by Jacqui Rivers
Printed and bound in Great Britain by Bath Colourbooks, Glasgow

Acknowledgements

The authors and publishers would like to thank the following for the use of copyright material:

Scriptures from the *Good News Bible* published by The Bible Societies/HarperCollins Publishers Ltd., UK, © American Bible Society, 1966, 1971, 1992 on pp. 19, 62; Extracts from *The Alternative Service Book 1980* are copyright © The Central Board of Finance of the Church of England, 1980; The Archbishops Council, 1999 and are reproduced by permission on pp. 53, 56, 57, 64; V P Hemet Kanitkar, *Hindu Festivals and Sacraments,* The Author, Barnet, 1984 for the extract on p. 10; The Muslim Educational Trust for the quotes from *Islam: Beliefs and Teachings* by Ghulam Sarwar, 1992 on pp. 66, 67, 76, 78, 79; By permission of Gerald Duckworth and Co Ltd, the extract from *Sayings of Muhammad* by N Robinson on p. 72; Scripture quotations are from the Revised Standard Version of the Bible, copyright 1946, 1952, 1971 by the Division of Christian Education of the National Council of the Churches of Christ in the USA. Used by permission on pp. 20, 33; Routledge for the extract from *The Sikhs: Their Religious Beliefs and Practices* by W O Cole and Piara Singh Sambhi on p. 90; Extract reproduced with permission from *Buddhism in the Twentieth Century* by Peggy Morgan © Stanley Thornes (Publishers) Ltd on p. 46; Reproduced by permission of the Union of Liberal and Progressive Synagogues. From *Siddur Lev Chadah*, 1995 © UPLS. Page 548, the extract on p. 22; United Synagogue for the extracts from *The Authorized Daily Prayer Book of the United Hebrew Congregations of the Commonwealth* on pp. 24, 30.

The publishers would like to thank the following for permission to use photographs:

Andes Press Agency pp. 49, 52, 55 (right), 57, 72 (bottom); Brian and Cherry Alexander p. 56 (top); Mark Azavedo pp. 10 (right), 44, 54, 56 (bottom), 66 (bottom) Robin Bath pp. 42 (top), 47 (bottom); Circa pp. 6, 14, 31 (top), 45, 53, 60 (both), 69, 70 (bottom), 81 (bottom), 83 (top), 84, 85, 86, 89; Corbis p. 27; Lupe Cunha p. 5; Eye Ubiquitous pp. 59, 93; Sally and Richard Greenhill pp. 15, 16 (both), 17; Sonia Halliday pp. 33 (top), 62 (bottom); Hutchinson Photo Library pp. 7 (top), 9 (top), 11, 26 (bottom), 29, 34, 35 (bottom), 80; Christine Osborne pp. 10 (left), 37, 39, 55 (left), 68 (top), 76, 90, 91, 93 (top); Pianos Pictures pp. 7 (bottom), 12, 40, 41, 49 (top), 62 (top), 73, 74 (top), 83 (bottom); Ann and Bury Peerless p. 20 (top); Peter Sanders pp. 68 (bottom) 70 (top), 71, 74 (bottom), 79 (both); Travel Ink pp. 4, 18; Trip Photo Library pp. 8, 9 (bottom), 13, 19, 20 (bottom) 21, 22, 23 (both), 24, 25 (both), 26 (top), 28, 30, 31 (bottom), 32, 33 (bottom), 35 (top) 36, 38, 42 (bottom), 43, 46, 47 (top), 50, 51, 58, 61, 63, 64, 65, 66 (top), 67, 7 (top), 75, 77, 78, 81 (top), 82, 87 (both), 88, 92.

The publishers wish to thank Panos Pictures/Nic Dunlop, Hutchison Library/Liba Taylor, Peter Sanders, Format Photographers/Judy Harrison and Zefa Picture Library for permission to reproduce the cover photographs.

The publishers have made every effort to trace the copyright holders, but if they have inadvertently overlooked any, they will be pleased to make the necessary arrangements at the first opportunity.

Tel: 01865 888058 www.heinemann.co.uk

Contents

1 Life maps

Many things in life are not certain. But two things are certain in every life. There is a beginning and there is an end.

There are questions to ask about these two things. For example, is our birth when we begin to exist or did we exist before? Is death the end of life or is there life after death?

People have different answers to these questions. They have different beliefs about the meaning of life too. Some say life has a definite plan and purpose. Others say it is up to us to find its meaning.

Making changes

To some extent our life is mapped out for us. There are things we cannot change - the way we look, our family, our culture.

But in some ways we can shape our lives. We can try to fulfil our hopes and ideals. We can learn a lot or a little. We can be content to let life go by or we can try to make changes.

A As we get older we may see life differently from the way we see it now

school is an important turning point. The turning points of life are times when we think about where we are going (**B**).

Special ceremonies

Each religion has special ceremonies to mark important stages and turning points in life. Although the ceremonies are different, they all make us think about where we are going. They remind us of our responsibilities and the choices we have to make.

Discussion question

What things can stop people from making changes they want in their lives?

Milestones

We can look at life in different ways. When we get older we may see life differently from the way we see it now (**A**). When we are young life seems to go on for ever. But we can see **milestones** on the way ahead. For example, leaving

3 The turning points in life make us stop and think

THINGS TO DO

1 Draw a diagram to show the way you see life. For example, is life like a board game or like a journey? You could use diagram **C** to help you.

2 'I want to be an astronaut when I grow up.' Have you changed your ideas about life? Write two sentences about how you once saw your life. Write a few more sentences about how you now see your life ahead.

3 How do you think the person in the photo (**A**) sees his life? Write a poem from the point of view of someone who is 64.

4 What do you think is the main difference between a religious person's view of life and the view of a non-believer? Write your answer in full sentences.

New words

milestones

C Some people see life as a journey

2 Hinduism: stages in life

Hindus believe that this life is one of many. They believe that everyone has a soul. They call this **atman**. The soul lives on after the body dies. It enters a new body and a new life. This life is only part of a much longer journey.

Discussion question

If you believed that this life is one of many would you think it was less important?

Stages in life

The Hindu scriptures say that life falls into stages called **ashramas** (**A**). These stages are important for different groups in society: the priests or **Brahmins**, the warriors or **Kshatriyas** and the merchants or **Vaishyas**. The stages of life are:

1 the student stage
2 the householder stage
3 retirement
4 the time of giving up worldly things.

The way to moksha

The first stage is a time of learning. This stage is before earning a living and bringing up a family get in the way. The second stage begins with marriage. This is when there is a home and family to look after. The third stage comes at retirement. Then there is time to read the scriptures and to go to the temple to pray. The last stage is at the end of life's journey. This is a time to give up the comforts of life to meditate and practise **yoga**. Each stage in life is a step on the way to **moksha**. Moksha is when the soul is freed from being reborn and finds union with God.

Duties in life

With each stage in life there are duties. These are called **dharma** (**B**). It is important to complete the dharma of one stage before starting on another. For example, students should work hard. They should not have relationships that will distract them.

With everyone doing their duty, the needs of the whole community are served. In this way everyone is able to make progress on their journey towards moksha.

A Some of the stages in life are shown in this family

B The householder must look after the religious life of the family

New words

atman   ashramas   Brahmins
Kshatriyas   Vaishyas   yoga
moksha   dharma

THINGS TO DO

1 Look at photo **A**. Choose one person. Imagine you are interviewing them. Ask them about their stage in life. Write up the questions and answers.

2 How do you see the different stages of life? Draw a picture to show them. Say what these stages are and describe the duties of each stage.

3 People have different needs. Look at photo **C**. This young person wants an education. Who must do their duty or dharma to ensure that his needs are met? Discuss your views in class and then write your own answer.

4 Divide a page into two columns. In the left column write down the following: student, husband, wife, grandmother, grandfather. In the right column write down duties and responsibilities of these people. For example:

Person	Duties
Student	Learning

C Whose dharma or duty is it to make sure he gets an education?

3 Before birth

The religious rituals which mark the stages in life in Hinduism are called **samskar**. Most religious traditions have a special ceremony to mark the birth of a child. In Hinduism the first samskar is performed by the husband and wife before the wife is pregnant. Once they are sure that the wife is pregnant there are special rituals for her.

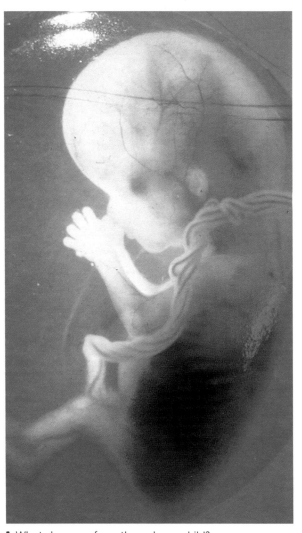

A What dangers face the unborn child?

Discussion question

What dangers face the unborn child (**A**)? What can the pregnant woman do to make sure the baby is safe?

Women celebrate

Between the fourth and seventh month of pregnancy, the female relatives in a Hindu family perform a special ceremony. They bring flowers to put around the neck of the mother-to-be and they **anoint** her with perfume.

She is offered tempting foods to satisfy her cravings. The women sing traditional songs and share a meal. Prayers are said for the safety and protection of the child.

During the pregnancy the parents-to-be offer gifts at the shrine. They pray for the welfare of the baby.

In some homes a fire ceremony called **Havan** is held (**B**). **Ghee** (clarified butter), sweet-smelling incense and rice grains are sprinkled on the flames.

Birth is rebirth

Hindus believe that the soul lives many lives on earth. Birth is rebirth. The soul carries **karma** from the previous life.

Karma is the effects of actions. Good actions bring good karma and bring good fortune. Selfish or evil actions bring bad karma and cause suffering.

New words

samskar   anoint   Havan   ghee   karma

B The fire ritual, called Havan, is a part of many Hindu ceremonies

C What hopes and fears will the mother-to-be have for her child?

Birth ceremonies

When a baby is born it needs washing. Today the midwife or hospital staff wash the baby. In the past the priest washed the child. Nowadays he will perform a symbolic cleansing. He sprinkles the mother and baby with drops of water and says prayers for their safety.

Once the baby has been washed (**A**), the mother is ready to see visitors. Close family come to offer congratulations.

Prayer for protection

When the father holds the baby for the first time he may perform a ritual to protect the child. He dips a gold ring into some honey and ghee and touches the baby's lips with the sweet mixture. He then prays:

> 'Oh dear child, I give you this honey and ghee which has been provided by God.... May you be protected by God and live...for a hundred autumns.'

Discussion question

What do you think the gold and honey might stand for in this ritual?

The naming ceremony takes place twelve days after the birth. The baby is washed and dressed in new clothes. It is laid in a cot which is surrounded by ghee lamps.

A When a child is born it needs washing. There are special rituals to do with this task

B 'May you be protected by God'

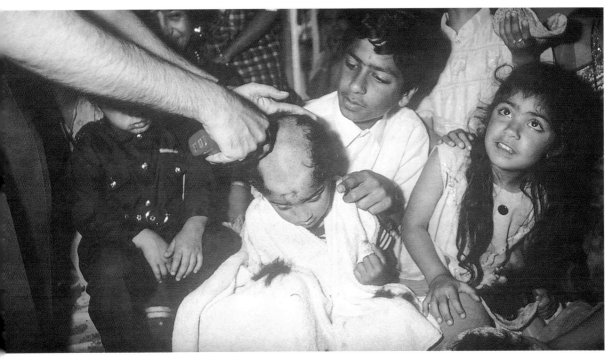

The child's first haircut is a special occasion

he priest calls out the name that has been hosen by the family so that everyone ears. They share sweetmeats and say rayers. Everyone sings hymns of praise efore joining in a festive meal. In some milies the baby's ears are pierced and old earrings are given.

)ther special occasions

nother ceremony takes place when the aby is first taken out into the sunlight. he father holds the child and recites the ;ayatri mantra (**B**). This is the daily rayer of every Hindu:

'Let us meditate on the Universal Divine Light, may it light up our thoughts and our prayers.'

lindu families have other ceremonies uring the early stages of the child's life. he first haircut is a special occasion (**C**). he first time the baby takes solid food is time for celebration too.

THINGS TO DO

1 Write three sentences to describe what happens when a Hindu child is born.

2 Draw the symbols of gold and honey and say how these play a part in the rituals celebrating the birth of a Hindu child.

3 There are many special events in the early life of the child. What do you think are important events from birth to the first day at school? Design a chart of these events for parents. Say why you have chosen these special events

4 Write a diary entry of a mother or father with a newborn child. Say how they feel a sense of responsibility.

New words

Gayatri mantra

5 The Sacred Thread ceremony

The Hindu scriptures say that when a boy is old enough he should begin to study with a religious teacher or **guru**. There is a special ceremony when the boy enters the student stage and receives the sacred thread. The sacred thread is worn by men in the Brahmin, Kshatriya and Vaishya classes (see Unit 2). The **Sacred Thread ceremony** is usually held when the boy is seven or eight. But it may be later when he is twelve.

Spiritual education

In the past, a Hindu boy left home to stay with his guru for his education. Today boys receive their general education at school (**A**). They then receive their spiritual or religious education from a guru.

The guru will help each boy to read the scriptures. He will also teach them how to meditate and to perform important religious rituals.

Discussion question

At what age does a young person really understand their religion? Discuss your ideas.

A special occasion

The Sacred Thread ceremony takes place at the boy's home. Friends and relatives are invited. Sometimes the boy's head is shaved for the ceremony. He bathes and puts on clean clothes. On the day he may fast until after the ceremony.

The priest lights a fire in a container. This

A Hindu boys get their general education at school

B The guru promises to be as a father to the boy

epresents the presence of God. The priest makes offerings of ghee and grains into the flames. He says prayers to the different gods. The boy and his father sit at the fire while the priest performs the ceremony.

Promises

Before he receives the sacred thread, the boy promises to be a good student. He also promises to be celibate (avoid sexual activities) until his studies are complete.

The guru promises to be as a father to the boy (**B**). He puts the sacred thread over the boy's head. It rests on the left shoulder and hangs diagonally across his chest. The thread has three strands joined with a sacred knot. The priest says the Gayatri mantra (see Unit 4) which the boy repeats after him. After the ceremony there is a celebration and the boy receives gifts.

New words

Guru   Sacred Thread ceremony

THINGS TO DO

1 Answer the following questions in sentences. Who wears the sacred thread? When does the Sacred Thread ceremony take place? Which stage in life does the Sacred Thread ceremony mark?

2 Write three questions asking what happens at the Sacred Thread ceremony. Then write three answers to the questions.

3 What important threads run through our lives? For example, do daily routines, family and friends hold our lives together? Write about the threads that hold your life together.

4 What special symbol do you think a young person should wear to remind them of their duties and responsibilities? Draw your symbol. In two sentences say what it means.

6 Finding a marriage partner

The second stage in the Hindu's life is the householder stage. This stage begins with marriage. For Hindus, marriage is a holy union between two people. It is an opportunity for them to grow together in mind and soul (**A**).

Perfect man and wife

The Hindu scriptures say that the god **Vishnu** came to earth as Rama. Prince Rama had to go into exile in the forest. His wife Sita gave up the comforts of the palace to be with him. In the forest Sita was kidnapped by the tyrant **Ravana** who took her to the island of Lanka. He tried to persuade her to give up her love for Rama. Sita remained faithful.

Eventually Rama killed Ravana and rescued Sita. Rama and Sita returned as king and queen. Rama was the perfect husband and Sita the perfect wife (**B**). Each was true to their dharma (duty) (see Unit 2).

Discussion question

What qualities would you look for in the perfect husband and perfect wife?

Finding a partner

Hindu marriage is not usually the result of two people meeting by chance and falling in love. Finding the right marriage partner is seen as too important to leave to chance. Hindu parents feel it is their duty to find a marriage partner for their son or daughter. Most young Hindus look to their parents to help them in this important step in life.

A For Hindus marriage is a time to grow together in mind and soul

B Rama and Sita represent the perfect husband and wife for Hindus today

Hindu parents may look for a suitable partner among their friends and contacts. They look for someone from a similar background - someone who will make a loving, caring partner. They take account of age, education and employment.

When the parents find someone suitable, a meeting is arranged. If the young person is not happy with their choice they usually wait until a suitable partner is found.

When a Hindu marries, he or she is joining a family. Everyone must be happy with the match. Once the couple is ready, a priest is contacted to arrange a date. The girl's family do all the preparations for the wedding.

New words

Vishnu   Ravana

THINGS TO DO

1 Design a cover for a booklet on Hindu marriage. Use Rama and Sita to show the perfect husband and wife.

2 Write answers to the following questions in full sentences. What does marriage mean for Hindus? How do Hindus usually find a marriage partner? What do the parents look for in a partner for their son or daughter?

3 What new responsibilities does a person have when they get married? Write down three responsibilities and explain them.

4 Love may come after the wedding in the Hindu marriage. Write a poem about love coming after marriage.

7 The wedding

The Hindu bride is the centre of attention on her wedding day. Her mother, sisters and female relatives help her prepare for the ceremony. This is a special time for the bride as she will leave her mother's home to start a new life with her husband.

Consent

In India the marriage is held at the home of the bride's family. In the UK it may be at the local Hindu temple. The wedding begins once the bride has given her consent to accept the groom. The father places her hand in the hand of the groom. The couple receive presents and gifts of money.

The sacred fire

The priest prepares the sacred fire. The couple face the fire, sitting side by side (**A**). A mark of coloured powder is put on the forehead of the bride and groom. This shows that they are taking part in a

B A prayer is said with each step around the sacred fire

religious ceremony. The bride may wear a red dot (**tilak**). This is a sign of being married.

The priest makes offerings to the gods. He asks them to bless the occasion. The couple repeat prayers said by the priest. They sprinkle a mixture of ghee and grains into the flames of the fire as an offering to God.

Discussion question

What are the similarities between this Hindu wedding and other wedding ceremonies you know about?

Seven steps

The wife and groom are joined with a symbolic knot using a silk scarf. Together they take seven steps beside the sacred fire (**B**). With each step a prayer is said –

A The couple sit together facing the sacred fire

C Giving each other sweet things to eat stands for the sweetness of the union

for strength, health, happiness, children, pleasure, long life and close union.

At the end of the ceremony the bride and groom give each other a cake (**C**). This stands for the sweetness of their union. It shows they will provide for each other.

After the ceremony there is a festive meal for friends and family. In India the celebrations may go on for several days.

2 Imagine you went to a Hindu wedding with a Hindu friend. Write six sentences describing what you saw when you were there.

3 Write down seven hopes or promises you think a couple could say when taking seven steps at the wedding ceremony.

4 What are the different feelings that people have at a wedding? Choose two people from a Hindu wedding ceremony and say what they might be feeling.

THINGS TO DO

1 Design an invitation to a Hindu wedding. Use some of the symbols of the ceremony in your design. Give details of the main events of the day.

New words

tilak

Preparing for death

Hindus believe that the third stage in life is retirement. This stage begins when the children have grown up. Then there is time to study the scriptures, visit the temple or go on pilgrimage.

In the UK many Hindu temples arrange transport for their senior citizens so that they can get to the temple every day. It is often the retired members of the community who take care of the temple.

Spiritual seeker

There is a fourth stage in life which some Hindus take up. This is the stage of the **sannyasin** or spiritual seeker. The sannyasin gives up the comforts of home and possessions. The aim is release from the cycle of rebirth and union with God (moksha).

The sannyasin lives a life of fasting, meditation, teaching and travelling. In this way he becomes free from karma and reaches moksha when he dies.

Discussion question

How does travelling with few possessions help to prepare you for death?

Cremation

Hindus cremate their dead. In the fire the body turns to ashes. They believe the soul is free to move on to the next stage in its journey. It will either reach moksha (union with God) or return to live in another body. In India **cremation** takes

A In India the body is laid on wood by the banks of a river

place near the banks of a river (**A**). In the UK a **crematorium** is used.

When a Hindu dies the body is washed and anointed. It is wrapped in a clean white cloth. In India the body is laid on firewood outside. Friends and relatives gather around (**B**). The eldest son lights the wood and the priest offers ghee and incense into the flames. He says prayers from the scriptures:

'Dear departed one, may your sight return to the sun and your soul be released – to return to the earth to enter a new body or to enter the realms of light.'

The ashes

Later the ashes are scattered on the waters

of a nearby river. Many Hindus take the ashes to the **River Ganges**. The waters of the Ganges are very sacred. Hindus believe that they can wash away all karma and help the soul reach moksha.

THINGS TO DO

1 Write down three things that you think social workers need to know if they are helping a Hindu family deal with the death of a loved one.

2 Many people save up for old age or have pensions. Write down two ways in which a Hindu prepares for death. Think of ways which are different from saving up money.

3 Fire, air and water are all elements. Draw each element and explain in a sentence how it plays a part in the Hindu funeral ceremony.

4 Moksha is release from the cycle of rebirth. It is perfect peace and pure happiness. Draw your image of perfect happiness and peace.

New words

sannyasin   cremation   crematorium
River Ganges

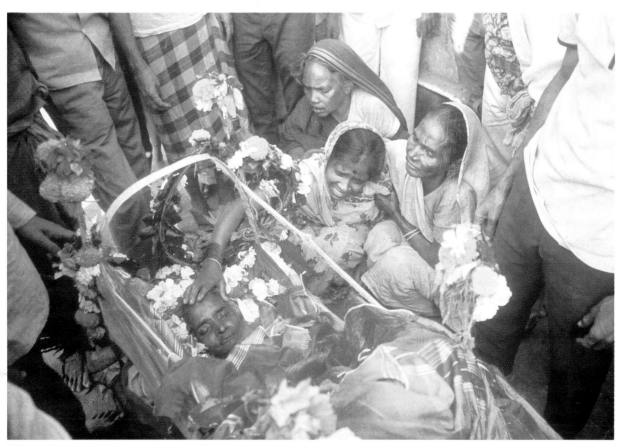

B 'Dear departed one, may your soul be released'

9 Judaism: the seasons of life

The Jewish scriptures are called the Torah (**A**). Here it says that God created man and woman. In **Genesis** there is a story about creation. It ends with a reminder that we will all die and become like dust:

'You are dust and to dust you shall return.'
(Genesis 3.19)

So life begins and ends according to God's will.

Discussion question

People like to think that they are in control. What does Genesis say about this?

A The Torah scrolls are held up in the synagogue

B This is the Jewish harvest festival of **Sukkot**

The Torah

The teachings of the Torah say that God wanted people to enjoy and benefit from his creation. Men and women were asked to look after God's world. They were also told to grow in number and to build up the human family on earth.

Seasons and celebrations

The cycle of the Jewish year is marked with festivals. These are times when Jews remember God's goodness and give thanks for his creation (**B**). There are times of joy and feasting. There are times for being serious and saying sorry.

Seasons of life

In the same way, there are celebrations for the different seasons of life. The teachings of the Torah say that human life begins at birth. Special blessings are said when a child is born. When a Jewish boy is thirteen there is a celebration at the **synagogue**.

C The huppah is a sign of togetherness

Marriage is the beginning of another season in life. The ceremony for this takes place under a canopy called a **huppah** (**C**). When a person dies there are important rituals to do and prayers to be said.

Special times in the life of the individual are also important times for the whole community. They are times to bring the teachings of the faith into everyday life.

THINGS TO DO

1 In the story of Genesis it says men and women will not live forever. Is it a good thing to live forever? Write down two advantages and two disadvantages.

2 'You are dust and to dust you shall return.' Write a poem with this line in it.

3 What are the different seasons of life? Make a poster to show this idea that life has seasons.

4 The Jewish way of life shows us that there are many moments in everyday life when we should celebrate – for example when we smell the scent of a flower or taste the new fruits of the season. Write down three things that happened this week when there was cause to celebrate.

New words

Torah   Genesis   Sukkot   synagogue   huppah

10 The path to holiness

In the Torah, there is a story where God makes a **covenant** or agreement with the people of Israel.

God promised to take care of his people. In turn they promised to keep God's laws:

'You shall be holy, for I the Lord your God am holy.'

(Leviticus 19.1)

For Jews, every occasion in life is a time to take a step towards being holy.

Good and evil

Jews believe that we have two opposite drives in us. One is the drive to do good. The other is the drive to do evil.

The ceremonies and celebrations of the religion encourage people to do good. By carrying out acts of kindness a person can also become holy.

Discussion question

What acts of kindness might be steps towards being holy?

Genesis

In the book of Genesis man and woman are told to:

'Have many children so that your descendants will live all over the earth.'

(Genesis 1.28)

A Having a family is a way of doing God's will

The Torah says that having children is a way of carrying out God's laws (**A**). It can be a step towards being holy. When a child is born into a Jewish family this blessing is said:

'We praise you, Eternal God, Lord of the Universe, that you have kept us alive, and have brought us to his season.'

When a girl is born

There are different rituals for boys and girls in the Orthodox community. When a girl is born the father is called up to say the blessings in the synagogue (**B**). Prayers are said for the baby and the name is announced.

In some Jewish communities, the women have their own ceremonies to celebrate the birth of a girl (**C**).

A Jewish child is given a Hebrew name. Often the first name is that of a relative. The surname is taken from the father. Every child born of a Jewish mother is Jewish. So being Jewish comes through the woman. The name comes through the father.

3 The father is called up to say the blessings in the synagogue

C Some Jewish women have special ceremonies for
he birth of a girl

THINGS TO DO

1 Write three sentences to explain the agreement made between God and his people in the Torah.

2 Divide a page in two. On one side write down the good things about having a family. On the other side write down things that people might say are bad. Write down what a Jewish person would say.

3 Do you think that good and evil are pulling us in different directions? Show this idea in a drawing or diagram.

4 Is a new baby a big change like a new season in life? Write down the changes that will take place in everyday life when a couple has a baby.

New words

covenant

11 Brit Milah

In the Torah it says that every Jewish boy must be circumcised on the eighth day after he is born. **Circumcision** is a sign of God's agreement with the Jews (see Unit 10). The prayer for the circumcision ceremony says:

> *'Blessed are You, Lord our God, King of the Universe .... you have commanded us to bring our sons into the Covenant.'*

Circumcision

Brit Milah means the 'covenant of cutting'. Covenant means agreement. Circumcision is the cutting and removal of the foreskin on the boy's penis. This is carried out by a trained **mohel** (**A**). Circumcision is very important. Only if the baby is unwell is Brit Milah delayed.

At Brit Milah, the father, the mohel and the **sandek** are present. The sandek is a male relative or friend who holds the baby during the ceremony. The mother does not attend the ceremony. However, she will be at the festivities afterwards.

Elijah

There is always an empty chair at Brit Milah (**B**). This is a sign of the prophet Elijah. The father does not hold the baby. He says the blessings. Once the circumcision is done someone dips their

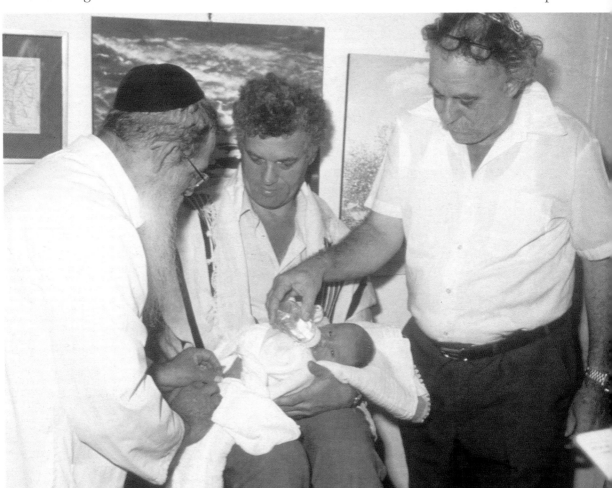

A Circumcision is a sign of God's agreement with the Jews

B The empty chair is left for the prophet Elijah

finger into sweet red wine to give a taste to the baby. Relatives and friends are then invited to celebrate at the family home (**C**).

Discussion question

Wine is an important part of many Jewish ceremonies. What do you think it means?

Circumcision is an outward sign of being Jewish but it is a personal one. It is a mark of the importance of the agreement between God and his people.

THINGS TO DO

1 Write three sentences in answer to these questions. What does the Torah say about circumcision? What does Brit Milah mean? How can you tell that Brit Milah is very important for Jews?

2 Look at photo A. Write three or four sentences to explain who is in the photo and what is happening.

3 Brit Milah links Jews with their history. What ceremonies or celebrations link you with the history of the community you live in? Write about one of these.

4 Brit Milah is not an easy time for the parents. Write a diary entry of either the mother or father on the evening after Brit Milah of their baby son.

New words

circumcision   Brit Milah   mohel
sandek

C Family and friends celebrate after the ceremony

12 Bar Mitzvah

Bar Mitzvah means 'Son of the Commandment'. A Jewish boy becomes Bar Mitzvah when he is thirteen and one day. From that day he is an adult in the eyes of the Jewish community.

Discussion question

In what ways do we mark the beginning of adulthood under UK law? At what age does the young person take on new responsibilities?

Classes

Before he becomes Bar Mitzvah, the Jewish boy goes to classes at the synagogue. These are given by the **rabbi** (**A**). In this way he learns about his new responsibilities. He is shown how to wear **tefillin** and **tallit** for prayer. He also has to

B This boy is celebrating his Bar Mitzvah in Jerusalem

study the scriptures.

Before his Bar Mitzvah the Jewish boy learns to read a passage from the Torah (**B**). The reading is in Hebrew. Many Jewish boys learn Hebrew from an early age. The rabbi will explain the meaning of the reading. He will also teach the boy to chant the words correctly.

Reading from the Torah

The Jewish boy is called to read from the Torah on the Saturday morning following his thirteenth birthday. He goes up to the platform called the **bimah** and chants the reading. He does this in front of all his friends and family.

When the reading is finished the father says:

> 'Blessed is He who has released me from responsibility for this child.'

A A Jewish boy studying with the rabbi

rom then on it is the boy's responsibility ɔ follow the teachings of the Torah and to ɪke care of his own religious education.

ᴧs an adult in the Jewish community he ɣill be able to make up the **minyan**. This ɪ the correct number of men to be able to ɣorship at the synagogue.

ᴧfter the service at the synagogue family nd friends gather for a celebration (**C**). he boy receives congratulations and ɪresents.

How does a Jewish boy prepare for his Bar Mitzvah ceremony?

2 What do most parents want for their children when they reach the age of thirteen? What do you think the Jewish parents will want for their thirteen-year-old boy? Discuss your answers in class. Write your answers in full sentences.

3 Jews believe it is good to study and learn. Why is it good to learn? Design a poster encouraging young people to take their studies seriously.

4 Growing up is something to celebrate. Write a song or poem which celebrates the good things about growing up.

THINGS TO DO

1 Write your answers to these questions. What does Bar Mitzvah mean? When does a Jewish boy become Bar Mitzvah?

New words

Bar Mitzvah   rabbi   tefillin   tallit
bimah   minyan

After the synagogue service family and friends gather for a celebration

13 Bat Mitzvah

Bat Mitzvah means 'Daughter of the Commandment'. A Jewish girl becomes Bat Mitzvah at the age of twelve.

The service in the synagogue takes place on or after her twelfth birthday.

Sometimes it is carried out for a group of girls all reaching this age at about the same time.

Reading from the Tenakh

Girls celebrating Bat Mitzvah read a passage from the Jewish scriptures (**A**). In an Orthodox synagogue this is not from the Torah. It is from another part of the Jewish Bible or **Tenakh**. (The Tenakh is the Torah, the **Prophets** and Writings.)

Friends and relatives come to the ceremony. There is a party after the service.

Discussion question

What are the similarities and what are the differences between the celebration of Bar Mitzvah and Bat Mitzvah? (Look back to Unit 12 to help you.)

Learning Hebrew

Many Jewish girls, like Jewish boys, go to lessons in Hebrew. They learn to read the scriptures. Jewish girls also learn how to keep the **kosher** food laws and how to prepare for **Shabbat** and other festivals. These lessons are learnt at home (**B**).

Jewish women

Jewish women have to keep the same laws as Jewish men. But there are a few exceptions. For example, women do not have to wear the tefillin or the tallit for

A A Jewish girl reads a passage from the scriptures at her Bat Mitzvah

Young Jewish girls learn about the ways of their religion at home

rayer. In Orthodox communities these differences still stand. Some say it is because women are by nature more religious. They do not need something to remind them to pray. In some communities the women now do some of the rituals performed by men.

Bat Mitzvah is a time for thinking about new responsibilities that come with growing up. At Bat Mitzvah the Jewish girl becomes responsible for keeping the Jewish faith and following the law.

THINGS TO DO

1 Write answers to these questions in full sentences. When does a Jewish girl become Bat Mitzvah? What does the Jewish girl have to do at her Bat Mitzvah ceremony at the synagogue? Which holy book does the girl read from at the Bat Mitzvah ceremony?

2 Design a card which friends could give to a Jewish girl at her Bat Mitzvah. Try to show the meaning of the occasion in your design.

3 Learning how to do what is right is an important part of preparing for Bar Mitzvah and Bat Mitzvah. Write down five teachings about how to do what is right that you think every young person should learn as they grow up.

4 Design a special ceremony about growing up and taking on new responsibilities for young people who are not religious. Describe what will happen at the ceremony.

New words

Bat Mitzvah   Tenakh   Prophets
kosher   Shabbat

Marriage

Jews believe that God created everything. Having a family means that men and women can share in this act of creation. Getting married and having children is a way to become holy (see Unit 10). Marriage brings joy, security and comfort and is something to celebrate. It is also a serious matter.

The ketubah

In the Jewish faith marriage is an agreement or contract between two people. It is described as 'a covenant of love and companionship, of peace and friendship'. In Jewish marriage there is a contract. This is called the **ketubah**. It sets down the duties of the husband. This is signed by the groom (A).

The huppah

The marriage service usually takes place in the synagogue. A huppah or canopy is set up for the occasion. This is a symbol of the home the couple will share. The bride and groom stand under the huppah in front of the rabbi (**B**). He begins the ceremony with a blessing over a cup of wine:

> 'Blessed are You, Lord our God, King of the Universe, who has blessed us with His commandments, and who blesses his people, Israel, by the rite of the marriage canopy.'

Seven blessings

The bride and groom each take a sip from the cup. The groom puts a ring on the bride's finger and says:

> 'You are consecrated [made special] to me with this ring according to the faith of Moses and of Israel.'

The ketubah is then read out. Seven

A The ketubah is signed by the groom

B The bride and groom stand under the huppah

blessings or prayers are said. This is one of them:

> 'Give these, companions in love, great happiness, the happiness of your creation in Eden long ago. May Your children be worthy to create a Jewish home, that honours You and honours them.'

Discussion question

Wine is often a symbol of joy. What do you think it represents here?

The couple then have another sip from the glass of wine.

The service ends with the groom breaking the glass under his foot (**C**). It is a reminder that marriage is a serious matter.

Later there is a celebration meal with singing and dancing.

THINGS TO DO

1 Draw three symbols from the Jewish wedding ceremony. Write a sentence to explain the meaning of each one.

2 Imagine you have been to a Jewish wedding. In full sentences describe what happened and what you saw.

3 What difficult lessons do you think people have to learn when they marry someone? In three or four sentences say what a Jewish rabbi might say about this at the ceremony.

4 Do people realise marriage is a serious matter? Write down three things that are serious about getting married and three things that are happy or exciting.

New words

ketubah

C The groom breaks the wine glass

A Jewish funeral

Jews believe that life is a gift from God. It is to be celebrated and enjoyed. It is the duty of everyone to save life. But when death comes it is to be accepted as the will of God in these words:

'Hear O Israel, the Lord is our God, the Lord in One. The Lord He is God. The Lord he is God. The Lord he is God.'

Burial

In Orthodox communities the body is buried. Only some **Reform Jews** allow cremation.

The Jewish funeral should take place within 24 hours of death. The body is washed and wrapped in a white cloth and put in a wooden coffin. Family and friends go to the service at the grave. The rabbi says prayers as the coffin is laid in the ground. The burial ends with the **kaddish**. This is a prayer in praise of God and his goodness.

Mourning

After the burial there is a week of mourning called **shivah**. Close family stay away from work. Friends bring them food. The mirrors in the home are all covered. Members of the family make a small tear in their clothing as a sign of mourning (**A**)

They wear soft shoes about the house and light a candle.

On the anniversary of the death the family lights a candle in the synagogue. This day of remembering is called the **yahrzeit** (**B** and **C**).

Discussion question

Why do you think covering the mirror is a sign of mourning?

A After the funeral there is a time of mourning

Every year on the anniversary of the death, prayers are said

After death?

The Torah says that the body returns to dust. The spirit returns to God. Some Jews look forward to a day when God's kingdom will be set up on earth. This is called the **Messianic Age.** Others say we should not worry about what will happen after death. That should be left to God.

THINGS TO DO

1 Answer the following questions in sentences. How should Jews respond to death when it comes? When does the funeral take place? What happens at the funeral?

2 Draw examples of two ways in which Jews show their mourning in outward signs. Explain the meaning of these signs and symbols in full sentences.

3 Is it a waste of time trying to work out what happens after death? What do you think? Write down your answers ready to present in class.

4 Design two symbols that could be useful signs of mourning for non-religious people who do not want to have to explain why they are sad all the time.

New words

Reform Jews   kaddish   shivah
yahrzeit   Messianic Age

C A candle is lit on the anniversary of the death

Buddhism: outlook on life

There are different ways of looking at life. Some people see life as a gift. Others see life as a journey. The Buddhist way is shaped by three important teachings of the Buddha.

Discussion question

'Life is not a bowl of cherries.' What sayings have you heard about life and what do these sayings mean?

A Is it true that all life is unsatisfactory?

A cycle of rebirth

The first Buddhist teaching on life is that we are caught in a cycle of death and rebirth. After death we are reborn and life continues in another body. There is no end to this cycle.

The Four Noble Truths

The second important teaching is in the **Four Noble Truths**. This is that 'All life is suffering' (**dukkha**). In other words we are never totally happy. We are never happy because we always want or crave something (**B**). This craving is like a fire. The aim of the Buddhist is to put out this fire. When this is done then the way is open to **Nibbana**. Nibbana is perfect

Four Noble Truths

1. Life is unsatisfactory and full of suffering

2. We suffer in this way because we are always wanting

3. The answer to the problem is to stop the craving

4. The way to stop the craving is to follow 'the middle path'

● We are always wanting something more so we ~~c~~annot be happy!

~~p~~eace. It is freedom from the cycle of birth ~~a~~nd death.

There is no soul

~~T~~he third important teaching is that there ~~i~~s no soul or self. This is called the ~~d~~octrine of 'non-self' (**anicca**).

~~T~~he Buddha said there is no soul that ~~s~~urvives death. We all make the mistake of ~~t~~alking about 'I' or 'me' as if we had a fixed ~~s~~elf or soul. It is this mistake that makes ~~u~~s want things (**C**).

~~W~~anting or craving brings us back into the ~~c~~ycle of rebirth. If we give up the idea of ~~s~~elf we will stop wanting things and see ~~l~~ife in a new way.

There is no belief in an individual self or personal soul in Buddhism. So there are not many personal ceremonies and **rites of passage** in Buddhism.

THINGS TO DO

1 Write answers to these questions in full sentences. What cycle do Buddhists believe we are caught in? What is the meaning of dukkha? What is the meaning of anicca?

2 How many times have you used the words 'me', 'mine', 'my...' today? Write down examples in speech bubbles. What does this say about how we see life?

3 What do the photos say about life? Write your answer. Say whether these pictures support the view that all life is suffering!

4 Make a poster to show how there is always pressure to want things in this life.

New words

Four Noble Truths   dukkha   Nibbana
anicca   rites of passage

C Even wealth cannot guarantee happiness

Rites of passage

Some of the ceremonies we find in other religions do not appear in Buddhism. For example, there is no traditional Buddhist marriage ceremony. There is no rite of passage to mark the birth of a child.

The way to Nibbana

The aim of the Buddhist is to reach Nibbana. **Theravada** Buddhists follow a way of life that was set up by Gotama Buddha. This is found in the teachings of the **Eightfold Path**.

The best way to keep to the Eightfold Path is to enter the **Sangha**. This is the community of monks and nuns. Monks and nuns do not marry or run a household. They study, pray and teach others about Buddhism. So there are no traditional ceremonies for marriage or birth.

The lay community

The Buddhist community is made up of two groups of people. First there is the Sangha and then there is the **lay community**.

Lay Buddhists marry and have children. They support the Sangha by giving food to the monks and nuns (**A**).

In the lay community, local beliefs shape the way in which people celebrate birth.

The Eightfold Path

1. Right Understanding

2. Right Thought

3. Right Speech

4. Right Action

5. Right Livelihood

6. Right Effort

7. Right Mindfulness

8. Right Concentration

A Buddhist monks and nuns rely on the lay community for food

All life is suffering

Buddhists believe that birth brings suffering. Life is not perfect. So birth is not really something to celebrate. Birth is rebirth. Life is an endless cycle of becoming. Our senses make us want things.

Wanting makes us act. Actions have effects (**kamma**). Good actions bring good kamma and selfish actions bring bad kamma. If we build up good kamma we will come back into a better life. If we have bad kamma we will pay for it in the next life.

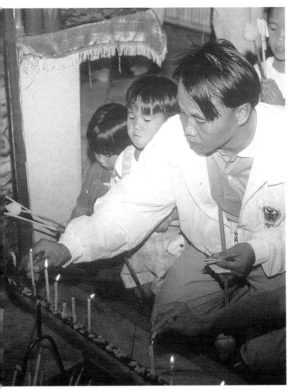

B After a child is born Buddhists may give thanks at a local shrine

In some places they make offerings to the local gods. They ask them to protect them from evil (**B**). They may also go to the temple (**vihara**) to receive blessings from the monks.

UK monastries

In the UK some Buddhist monasteries have a ceremony to mark the birth of a child. People take the baby to the monastery and make offerings at the shrine.

Discussion question

Why do you think that Buddhists in the UK want a ceremony to mark the birth of a child?

THINGS TO DO

1 Write two sentences to explain the difference between the life of the nuns and monks and the life of the lay people in Buddhism.

2 Draw a diagram to show that there is no end to life, death and rebirth in the Buddhist view of life. You could show birth as one link in a chain of births.

3 Write down three things that you think every parent would wish to protect their child from. Say how parents can protect their child.

4 What things shape our lives before we are born? Design a poster to show your ideas.

New words

Theravada   Eightfold Path   Sangha
lay community   vihara   kamma

18 Growing up in Buddhist society

Most parents want the best education for their children. In countries where most people are Buddhist, the temple is also a place of education. Some temples have classes in **Pali** or Sanskrit. These are the languages of the scriptures.

So lay Buddhists can learn to read the teachings of the Buddha. These are called **Dhamma**. The temple also offers lay Buddhists classes in **meditation**.

In many Buddhist countries the temples are schools for the children in the lay community (**B**). For monks and nuns the temple is always a place of learning.

Ordination

When someone wants to become a member of the Sangha they go through a special ceremony of **ordination**. There are different levels of ordination. Higher ordination is for those who want to find the path to Nibbana. Lower ordination is for lay Buddhists who join the Sangha for a short time. Later they return to the lay community.

In some Buddhist countries parents send their sons to spend a few months as members of the Sangha (see Unit 19).

A Temples provide classes on meditation

◄ Some temples provide education for the young

Discussion question

What would you learn from being in a Buddhist monastery for a short time?

Away from home

At the Sangha the boy gets his religious education. He learns about the teachings of the Buddha. This time of being away from home and family marks a new stage in his life. It may be the time between school and going into a job or higher education.

THINGS TO DO

1 Answer the following questions in full sentences. What classes can people do at a Buddhist temple? What do temples in Buddhist countries provide for the lay community?

2 Design a leaflet advertising the idea that young Buddhists should think about joining the Sangha for a few months.

3 Write down three ways in which staying away from home for three months could help a young person to grow up.

4 Taking time out between school and work is sometimes helpful. Say what you would like to do between school and work. Say how this will help you to grow up.

> **New words**
>
> Pali   Dhamma   meditation   ordination

⓵⓽ Initiation

In Buddhist countries there is a special ceremony when a young person joins the community of monks and nuns (Sangha). This ceremony is usually for boys. In some cases he is dressed in rich clothing like a prince (**A**). This is a reminder of the young Gotama Buddha. He gave up the life of a prince to become a holy man. The costume is later changed for the robes of the monk. These are provided by the parents or relatives. The family also takes food as a gift for the monks and nuns.

Entering the monastery

When the boy arrives at the temple he has his head shaved. This shows that he is giving up a life of comforts and possessions. It is a mark of poverty and self-control. He then takes his robes to the senior monk and bows before him (**B**). He kneels on the floor and asks permission to enter the life of a monk.

The senior monk gives a short sermon. This is based on the teachings of the Buddha. It reminds the young people that the things of this life cannot bring true happiness. All things change and pass away. The answer is to seek Nibbana. Only then will one find true happiness and overcome the cycle of rebirth.

Promises

The boy is dressed in saffron coloured (yellow) robes. The monk who will be his teacher takes him up to the senior monk. The boy promises to obey the teachings of the Buddha and the rules of the community.

The boy will learn about the life and

A The rich clothing is a reminder of the life Gotama Buddha left behind

B The young Buddhists take their saffron robes to the senior monk

teachings of the Buddha. He will also learn how to meditate. He will follow the daily routine of the Sangha. This begins before dawn.

The Ten Precepts

In the temple there are **Ten Precepts** or rules for living that the young Buddhist will have to keep:

1 To not kill or injure living things
2 To not take what is not given
3 To avoid any sensual misconduct
4 To avoid lying and wrong speech
5 To avoid taking alcohol or misusing drugs
6 To not eat anything after midday
7 To avoid taking part in entertainments such as dancing
8 To not use jewellery or perfumes
9 To not sleep in a luxury bed
10 To avoid handling money.

THINGS TO DO

1 Design a poster to teach the Ten Precepts to young Buddhists.

2 Write six sentences to explain what happens when a young Buddhist enters the monastery for a short time.

3 Change of clothes, hairstyle, daily routine – are these things that have changed as you have grown up? Write a magazine article about how life changes as you grow up.

4 Write your own Ten Precepts or rules for living that would be useful for young people growing up. Make sure they encourage young people to think about more than just having a good time.

New words

Ten Precepts

Marriage

Buddhist monks and nuns do not marry. Sometimes a married person joins the Sangha late in life. This is after they have done with their family responsibilities. They must have the agreement of their partner.

Buddhists value family life as important for the lay community. It gives balance and stability. The Sangha can only survive if there is a lay community to support it.

Following customs

There is no traditional Buddhist marriage ceremony. Usually local customs are followed (**A**). For example, in the UK a Buddhist couple may marry at the **registry office**.

B Buddhists in the UK go to the temple for a blessing on their marriage

Some temples now offer a religious blessing after the registry office wedding. This is carried out by a monk in the shrine room at the temple (**B**).

A Local customs are followed for weddings

Discussion question

Why do so many people feel that the registry office wedding is not enough?

Puja

At a ceremony at the temple, the couple attends **puja**. Offerings are made at the shrine of the Buddha. There is usually a sermon from one of the monks. This is to remind the couple of their responsibilities to one another. Man and woman are equal partners in Buddhism. Both must try to

C Family and friends take food to the monks and nuns to mark the special occasion

follow the teachings of the Buddha in their married life.

Shared food

Friends and family are invited to join the couple at the temple. Everyone takes food to prepare a meal for the monks and nuns (**C**). Later they join in a shared meal.

Married life

The life of the married couple is too full of the cares of work and family to lead to Nibbana. If the couple live by the teachings of the Buddha they may be reborn as a monk or nun. They can then make progress towards Nibbana.

THINGS TO DO

1 Answer the following questions in full sentences. Why does the community of monks and nuns need the lay community? Why do Buddhists value family life?

2 Design a card inviting friends and family to a UK Buddhist wedding. Explain why everyone must help with bringing food.

3 Write down three things that the Buddhist monk might say to the couple in a sermon when blessing the wedding.

4 Monks and nuns give up the comforts of married life. What will be the rewards? What will be the hard things about giving up on married and family life? Write your answers listing them in two columns.

New words

registry office   puja

21 Death is not to be feared

Buddhists say death is not an end. It is only a moment among many within the cycle of life and death. There is no soul or spirit that survives death. Only consciousness continues. When one life goes out another begins. It is like a candle, which lights the flame of another just before going out (**A**).

The Three Jewels

The **Three Jewels** help Buddhists on the path to Nibbana. These are:

- the Buddha
- the Dhamma (the Buddha's teachings)
- the Sangha

A One life ends and another begins like one candle lighting another

Every Buddhist tries to keep the Five Precepts:

1 To not harm living things
2 To not take what is not given
3 To avoid sexual misconduct
4 To not tell lies or say wrong things
5 To not take any intoxicating drugs.

Lay Buddhists who follow these guidelines will build up good kamma.

When they die they will be reborn into a better life. Therefore, there is no need to fear death.

Discussion question

If you knew you were going to be born again into a better life after death would you have a different attitude to death from the one you have now?

Nibbana

Monks and nuns follow the Eightfold Path (see Unit 17). If they have lived a life of loving kindness they will be close to Nibbana. If they have put an end to greed, hatred and ignorance they will be very close indeed.

Nibbana is a state of pure happiness and peace. It is the end of rebirth. So death is not to be feared.

Bodhisattvas

Mahayana Buddhists believe there are beings who help others to reach Nibbana. These beings have made a vow:

*'May I not enter Nibbana until I have brought all other beings to **enlightenment**.'*

B Bodhisattvas show endless compassion

Such beings are called **bodhisattvas** (B). They have endless kindness and help others to reach Nibbana.

THINGS TO DO

1 Answer the following questions in sentences. Why don't lay Buddhists who have kept the five precepts fear death? Why don't monks and nuns who have put an end to greed, hatred and ignorance fear death?

2 What is Nibbana? Write the question in the middle of the page. Write different answers around the word including the way to Nibbana.

3 If you are good you get good kamma. If you are selfish you get bad kamma. Make a board game based on this idea.

4 The Bodhisattva is a being of endless kindness. Show this idea in a poster.

New words

Three Jewels   Mahayana
enlightenment   bodhisattvas

Funeral rites

Buddhist funeral rites vary greatly from one community to another (**A**). To the outsider it may seem more like a festival than a funeral.

When a person in the lay community dies, the family looks after their body. It is washed carefully and laid in a wooden coffin. This is covered in flowers and carried to the temple. It is set out in the shrine room.

A Funerals vary from one community to another

Offerings of flowers are made at the shrine of the Buddha. Blessings are said:

*'Reverencing the Buddha we
    offer flowers.
Flowers that today are fresh
    and sweetly blooming.
Flowers that tomorrow are
    faded and fallen.
Our bodies too like flowers
    will pass away.'*

Discussion question

Flowers are often used in funerals. What do you think is the reason for this? What do they stand for?

A shared meal

After the ceremony at the shrine the senior monk reminds everyone of the teachings of the Buddha. The family and friends bring food for the monks and nuns and share a meal. It is not usual to show a lot of sadness. There is hope that the person who died will move on to a better life. Later the body is taken for **cremation**.

The death of a monk or nun

In some Buddhist communities there are very special ceremonies to mark the death of a monk or nun (**B**). A funeral tower is built for the coffin. It is brightly decorated and covered in flowers. This is carried in a procession with music to the cremation ground. After the cremation the ashes are collected up. They may be scattered into the waters of a lake or into the sea (**C**).

New words

cremation

Special ceremonies mark the death of a Buddhist monk or nun

After cremation the ashes are scattered

THINGS TO DO

1 Answer the following questions in full sentences. What happens when a lay Buddhist dies? What happens when a Buddhist monk or nun dies?

2 Write three questions that you would want to ask a Buddhist about their views on death. Write down the answers you think he/she might give.

3 Buddhist monks have to meditate on death. For example they may meditate on the way flowers decay. Write a poem or a meditation on the way flowers fade and die.

4 Flower, candles, prayers and music can help people show their feelings when someone dies. Suggest some of your own ideas for a ceremony to mark the death of a loved one.

23 Christianity: the journey of life

Many Christians see life as being like a journey (**A**). Christians believe that God guides and supports them through life. Like most journeys, life has turning points and **milestones** on the way.

These are times for Christians to reflect on their faith and to make a fresh start in life.

Discussion question

Can you think of an example of a milestone in life? For example, a birth or a death which has made people stop and think about life? What was the effect of the event?

The story of the talents

There was once a man who was going away. He put his servants in charge of his money. To one he gave five thousand silver coins. To another he gave two thousand. And to the third he gave one thousand. The first and the second servant invested the money wisely. They earned double the amount. The third dug a hole in the ground and hid the money.

When the master returned he asked each servant to tell him what they had done. The first said, 'Look, you gave me five thousand – I have doubled your money'. The master said ' You good and faithful servant. I will reward you.'

The second said, 'You gave me two thousand – here I have doubled it!' Again the master was pleased.

The third servant said, 'I hid your money in the ground – here it is.' The master said 'You bad and lazy servant. Why did you waste this opportunity? Give the money to the first servant.'

A Christians see life as a journey

B This painting shows Jesus teaching. Jesus told his followers they must not waste the gifts God had given them

A gift from God

Christians speak of life as a gift from God. This gift carries important responsibilities. In the story of the talents, Jesus tells his followers that they should not waste the gifts and talents they have been given in life (**B**).

New words

milestones

C We must use our talents well

THINGS TO DO

1 Many Christians say life is like a journey. What are the milestones and turning points in the life of a Christian? What are the things to guide and support them? Draw a diagram of the Christian idea of the 'journey of life'.

2 Act out the story of the talents in class. Write three sentences to explain the meaning of the story for someone to read out at the end.

3 What gifts and talents can a person have? Is it wrong to let these talents go to waste? Write two sides to a discussion. One side is the voice of a lazy person who does nothing. The other side is the voice of someone who is trying to follow the teachings of Jesus.

4 Life is a journey! Design and write a minibook for young children in which you tell your life as a journey.

Birth and baptism

The birth of a child, a wedding and the death of a loved one. These are times when people think about life and its meaning. For Christians, the rituals to mark these occasions are times for them to think about their own journey through life.

The birth of a baby is a time when the Christian community gives thanks to God. It is also a time when members of the church are called to think about their commitment to Christ.

The Orthodox Church

In the **Orthodox Churches** there are many ceremonies to mark the birth of a child. Prayers are said on the first day after the mother has given birth. On the eighth day after the birth there is a ceremony at the church. The baby receives its name and prayers are said for the child. Forty days

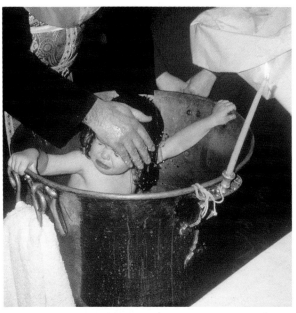

A In Orthodox Churches baptism means going right into the water

after the birth the mother brings the baby to be introduced to the church. Again prayers are said for the mother and child.

Infant baptism

To celebrate the arrival of a baby, many churches have a service of **infant baptism**. In the Orthodox Church **baptism** involves going right into the water (**A**). Godparents are chosen for the child.

The **priest** asks two questions which the godparents answer for the child. He first asks if they turn away from the **devil** and all his works. He then asks if they are ready to be united with Christ. These questions are asked three times. Then the baptism can go ahead.

Discussion question

What do you think it means to promise to 'turn away from the devil and all his works'? What can godparents do to keep the child away from the works of the devil?

The church is lit with candles. The priest says prayers:

> 'that s/he may prove to be a child of Light and receive God's blessings; let us pray to the Lord that s/he may grow and share in the life of Christ our Lord.'

The priest makes the sign of the cross with oil on the baby's forehead, chest and between the shoulders. The child is then covered in water three times. The priest says:

> 'In the name of the Father and the Son and the Holy Spirit.'

After the baptism the child is anointed with oil

After the baptism in water the child is dressed in a white robe and **anointed** with oil (**B**).

Symbols

Symbols are important in Christian baptism. The oil used is called the oil of gladness. Making the sign of the cross is a reminder of the death of Jesus Christ. Christians believe that through the death of Christ they are freed from sin and evil. Water is a symbol of the **Holy Spirit**. The Holy Spirit is the presence of God at work in the lives of those who follow Christ.

THINGS TO DO

1 Write a sentence under each heading to explain how birth is celebrated in the

Orthodox Church:
- The first day after the birth
- Eight days after the birth
- Forty days after the birth
- Infant baptism

2 Design a card to show three symbols that are important in the baptism service. Say what they mean.

3 What do people mean when they say life is a gift? Write a poem to show this idea.

4 Choosing the right name for a child is important. Write a short play in which a Christian family discusses a name for their new baby.

New words

Orthodox Churches infant baptism
baptism priest devil anointed
Holy Spirit

Infant baptism

There are different Christian Churches. In some churches members are baptized as babies. In other churches members have to be old enough to decide for themselves. The **Anglican** service of infant baptism takes place when there is an ordinary Sunday service.

At the baptism, the parents and godparents stand at the **font** with the **minister**. A candle is lit and given to one of the parents or godparents. The parents and godparents have to confirm their belief in God and Christ (**A**). They make promises for the child to follow and trust in Christ. It is the duty of the godparents to see that the child grows up in the Christian faith.

The baptism

The minister **consecrates** (blesses and makes holy) the water in the font. He gives thanks for the life of the child. Everyone is reminded of their commitment to follow Christ.

Discussion question

Then the parents are asked to name the child. The minister holds the baby and says the name. He scoops up a little water and pours it onto the child's forehead (**B**) saying:

> 'I baptize you in the name of the Father, the Son and the Holy Spirit.'

The minister makes the sign of the cross on the child's forehead and says:

> 'I sign you with the sign of the cross, the sign of Christ.'

A Parents and godparents confirm their belief in God and Christ

3 An Anglican minister pours water over the forehead of a baby

The Roman Catholic Service

The **Roman Catholic** service is very similar to the Anglican one. In both Churches godparents and parents make promises for the child.

After the ceremony there is a family celebration in the home with relatives and friends. In some households a special cake is served and presents are given to the child.

Dedication

Some Christians choose to have a **dedication** rather than a **christening** for their child. A dedication service is to give thanks to God for the birth of the baby. Later the child may be baptized when he or she is old enough to understand the meaning of Christian commitment.

New words

Anglican   font   minister
consecrates   Roman Catholic
dedication   christening

THINGS TO DO

1 Write a leaflet on baptism in the Anglican Church. Try to answer the following questions:
   • What is infant baptism?
   • What do the parents and godparents promise?
   • What does the priest or minister do and say?

2 Write an advertisement/job description for an ideal godparent. Make sure that it says they must bring the child up in the Christian faith.

3 Design a card that a godparent might send to the parents with hopes for the child's future.

4 Describe a ceremony you could have for the birth of a child in a non-religious family.

First Communion

In many Christian Churches there is a service where bread and wine are shared. It is called different things – **Holy Communion, Mass**, the **Eucharist**, the **Breaking of Bread** or the **Lord's Supper**. It celebrates the last supper Jesus held with his friends. In the Roman Catholic and Anglican Churches, taking Communion for the first time is an important step in the Christian journey of faith.

The Roman Catholic Church

In the Roman Catholic Church there is a celebration when children take their **First Communion**. This is usually when they are about seven. They prepare carefully for this. First they confess and say sorry for all the things they have done wrong. They must try to do better in the future.

Confession is important before taking Communion. In the **Bible**, Saint Paul says that everyone should look at themselves before sharing the bread and wine.

Some people ask the priest to hear their confession. Others prefer to make their confession in private prayer.

Discussion question

What do you think Saint Paul meant when he asked Christians to look at themselves?

Classes

Most children take classes before their First Communion (**A**). These are given by a priest. He explains the symbols of bread and wine and the meaning of the service.

A Children learn about the meaning of the bread and wine before their First Communion

B Boys and girls often wear their best clothes for their First Communion

Remembering Jesus' words

At their First Communion, children wear their best clothes (**B**). The priest invites them to come up to the **altar** to receive the **host** (**C**). The host represents the bread of the Last Supper. When Jesus broke the bread he said it was his body. When he shared the wine he said it was his blood. Christians remember these words at Holy Communion.

In some Churches there is no special service for First Communion. In the **Baptist** Church people share the bread and wine once they feel old enough to understand the meaning. In the Anglican Church, believers do not take Communion until they have been **confirmed** (see unit 27).

(see unit 27).

THINGS TO DO

1 Answer the following questions in full sentences: Which church has a service called First Communion? How do children prepare for this occasion? What do Christians remember when they take Communion?

2 Design a diagram or poster that the priest could use to explain the meaning of the bread and wine for Christians.

3 Tell a story about someone who has to say sorry for what they have done. Explain how they make an effort to be better in the future.

4 Write about a time when you got ready to do something for the first time. Say how you felt about the occasion.

New words

Holy Communion   Mass   Eucharist
Breaking of Bread   Lord's Supper
First Communion   confession   Bible
altar   host   Baptist   confirmed

C Receiving the bread and wine

Confirmation

The word confirmation means 'to make firm'. In some churches there is a special service where Christians make firm their commitment to follow Christ.

When a child is baptized as a baby it is the godparents who make promises for the child. At confirmation the Christian makes the promises for himself/herself.

Preparation

Before being confirmed, believers go to classes given by the priest or minister (**A**). They learn to deepen their faith through prayer, confession, Bible reading and service in the community. They also learn about the Church and the meaning of the scriptures.

Discussion question

What questions do you think a young person might ask at confirmation classes?

B Some **Protestant Churches** do not have bishops. The minister carries out the confirmation service

The Holy Spirit

In the Roman Catholic, Anglican and Orthodox Churches, confirmation is performed by a **bishop**. The priest or minister leads the service (**B**). The prayers and readings are about the Holy Spirit. Christians believe that God's gift of the Holy Spirit gives courage and strength to all who follow Christ.

At the Anglican confirmation service, Christians answer these questions:

- Do you turn to Christ?
- Do you **repent** of your sins?
- Do you renounce (give up) evil?

The bishop then asks three further questions.

A Young Christians go to classes to prepare for confirmation

- Do you believe and trust in God the Father, who made the world?
- Do you believe and trust in his Son Jesus Christ, who redeemed mankind?
- Do you believe and trust in his Holy Spirit, who gives life to the people of God?

The people being confirmed answer these questions. They kneel before the bishop. He places his hands on the head and says:

'Confirm, O Lord, Your servant with your Holy Spirit.'

Each one replies 'Amen'. In the Roman Catholic Church the bishop anoints them with oil (**C**).

New words

Protestant Churches   bishop
repent

THINGS TO DO

1 Design a poster to tell young people about confirmation classes that are being held at the church. Use photo **A** to help you. Say what might be discussed.

2 Use the following headings to write and explain what happens at confirmation:
   - Preparation
   - The service
   - Questions and answers
   - What the bishop does.

3 There are things which we need to confirm or 'say again'. For example saying what we believe, saying we love someone, reassuring someone. Describe a situation where someone has to confirm what they mean in this way.

4 Taking responsibility is a part of growing up. Write down five things you take responsibility for now which other people took care of when you were younger.

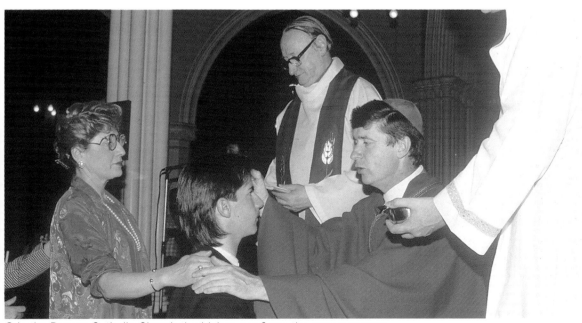

C In the Roman Catholic Church the bishop confirms the young person

Believer's baptism

In some churches there is no infant baptism. Members of the Baptist Church believe it is better to leave baptism until a person is old enough to decide their own faith.

They have a service called **believer's baptism**. It shows a full personal commitment to the faith.

Jesus' baptism

In the Bible, Jesus Christ commanded his disciples to baptize believers. Jesus himself was baptized in the River Jordan. Some Baptists today are baptized in the waters of the sea or in a river (**A**).

In the UK, most baptisms take place in a church.

Discussion question

What do you think are the advantages and the disadvantages of baptism in a) sea or river b) a church?

Believers who want to be baptized go to classes run by the minister. They learn about the meaning of baptism. They also think about the responsibilities of being a Christian.

The baptistry

In a Baptist church there is a pool called a **baptistry**. It is kept empty and covered when not in use. Baptisms are usually held during a normal Sunday service.

A Some Christians are baptized in the waters of the sea or river

B The believer is lowered into the water

The minister leads the worship. Those being baptized declare their faith. One at a time they step down into the baptistry.

When they are in the water the minister asks them:

> *'Do you confess Jesus Christ as your Saviour and Lord?'*

The believer says 'I do'. The minister then says:

> *'On your confession of faith in Jesus Christ as Saviour and Lord, I baptize you in the name of the Father, the Son and the Holy Spirit.'*

Then he lowers the believer backwards under the water for a brief moment and lifts him or her up again (**B**). Hymns are sung. Those who have been baptized change into dry clothes.

Going under the water symbolizes dying and rising again with Christ. It means leaving behind a selfish life and starting a new life with Christ. Some believe that the water represents the washing away of sin.

THINGS TO DO

1 Answer the following questions in sentences. What do Baptists believe about baptism? Where do most Baptists in the UK get baptized? What is the baptistry?

2 Write down five things that happen at a believer's baptism. Illustrate one of these.

3 Write down two arguments that a Baptist might give against infant baptism.

4 Baptism is often seen as a new beginning. What kind of new beginning would you like to see in your life?

New words

believer's baptism   baptistry

Marriage

Christians believe that marriage is a union of two people for life. Marriage is also for raising a family. Christians believe that God is involved in joining the two people in the marriage ceremony (**A**).

At the wedding ceremony in the Anglican Church the minister reminds everyone that:

> *'We have come together in the presence of God, to witness the marriage of (name) and (name) and to ask His blessing on them. The scriptures teach us that marriage is a gift of God in creation and a means of His grace, a holy mystery in which man and woman become one flesh.'*

B The bride and groom kneel before the minister

The service

The service includes hymns, prayers, readings from the Bible and usually a **sermon**. The minister asks if anyone knows of any reason in law why the couple should not be married. He names the groom and asks:

> *'Will you take (name) to be your wife? Will you love her, comfort her, honour and protect her and, forsaking all others, be faithful to her as long as you both shall live?'* (**B**)

The groom answers and the bride is asked the same questions. When both have made their vows they are asked to repeat after the minister:

> *'I take you, to be my husband/wife, to have and to hold from this day forward; for better for worse, for richer, for poorer, in sickness and in health, to love and to cherish, till death us do part, according to God's holy law; and this is my solemn vow.'*

A A couple getting married in an Orthodox Church

The ring

The groom puts the ring on his wife's finger. Sometimes the groom receives a ring from his bride (**C**). The bride and groom are declared to be man and wife by the minister who says:

'That which God has joined together, let no man divide.'

Discussion question

Many who are not church-going Christians want to marry in a Church. Should the Church agree to this?

New words

sermon

THINGS TO DO

1 Write out the statements which say what Christians believe about marriage:
   - Marriage is meant to be for life.
   - Marriage is a union of love.
   - Marriage does not matter.
   - Raising a family is an important part of marriage.
   - Marriage does not have to last.
   - God is involved in joining the couple in marriage.

2 Write three or four sentences about what happens at the Anglican wedding ceremony.

3 Design a wedding banner with a symbol to show the meaning of Christian marriage. Look at the words and symbols of the service to get ideas.

4 Design your own wedding ceremony. Draw or say which symbols you would have. Explain what promises would be made.

C The exchange of rings is a sign of unity

30

Death

Christians believe that Christ rose from the dead. This is called the **Resurrection**. They believe that Christ has overcome the power of death. Because of Christ's Resurrection, Christians believe everyone can share in the new life of Christ.

In the Bible, St Paul writes about the resurrection of the dead at the end of time:

'We shall not all die, but when the last trumpet sounds, we shall all be changed in an instant, as quickly as the blinking of an eye. For when the trumpet sounds, the dead will be raised.'

(1 Corinthians 15:51-53)

Reunited with God

Christians believe that we cannot know

B Christians believe that they should visit the sick or dying

exactly what happens after death. Some say that the physical body dies but that the dead will be raised in a spiritual body. Many Christians believe that when the body dies the soul survives and is reunited with God.

Roman Catholic beliefs

Christians who are Roman Catholics believe that the good go to **Heaven** (**A**). Those who are evil and reject God go to **Hell**. The rest who have sinned but who ask forgiveness go to **Purgatory**. This is to pay for their bad actions and prepare them for heaven.

Discussion question

What might be the difference between a physical body and a spiritual body?

When someone is very ill or close to death the priest or minister will visit them. They may pray with them (**B**). They may take them Holy Communion at the home or hospital. This is so that they can receive the bread and wine. They may listen to their concerns or just sit with them to comfort them.

Paying respects

When a person dies the body is washed

A Roman Catholics believe that the souls of the good go to heaven

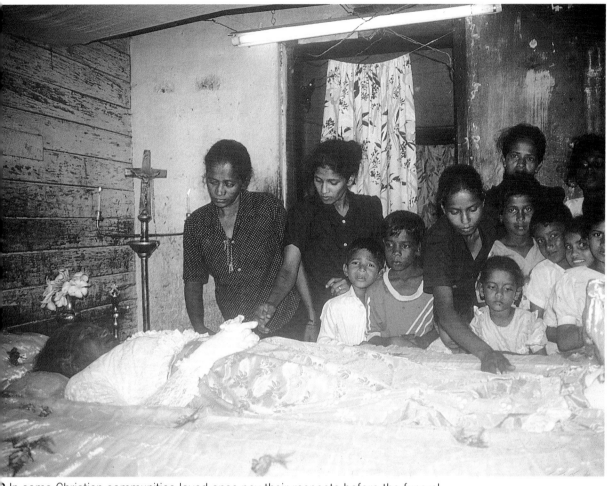

C In some Christian communities loved ones pay their respects before the funeral

ınd dressed and laid in a coffin. It may be
ept at a chapel or funeral parlour. It may
ɔe taken to the home of the family where
ɔrayers are said. In the Orthodox and
Roman Catholic Churches, the coffin is
ometimes left open until after the
uneral. This is so that people can pay
heir respects (**C**).

THINGS TO DO

1 Write answers to the following
questions. What do Christians believe
happened after the death of Christ?
How is it that people can share in the
new life of Christ? What did St Paul say
about the resurrection of the dead?

2 Write down three things that a church
minister or priest might do to offer
support to people who are very sick
or dying.

3 Design a poster to show some of the
beliefs about death mentioned in this
unit.

4 The cross might make Christians think
about death. Is it a good thing to think
about death sometimes? Write your
answer in full sentences.

New words

Resurrection   Heaven   Hell
Purgatory

31

The funeral

The Christian Church allows burial or **cremation**. The family tries to follow the wishes of the person who has died. They will also talk to the minister or priest of the church to which the person belonged. This is to make arrangements for the funeral. The person who has died may have chosen hymns and prayers for their funeral.

Discussion question

Some Christians leave very clear instructions about the kind of funeral they would like. Do you think this is a good idea? Why might this be helpful?

The service

The funeral service may take place at the **crematorium** (**A**) or the church. Prayers are said to thank God for the person's life. The minister offers words of comfort. Close friends or relatives may say a few words about the person who has died.

If the body is to be buried, people go to the graveside. The priest or minister says words from the Bible. These remind everyone of the promise of the resurrection (see Unit 30). The coffin is lowered into the ground. The minister scatters soil on the top of the coffin (**B**). He says:

'We commit (name's) body to the ground. Earth to earth, ashes to ashes, dust to dust.'

After the funeral

Friends and relatives leave flowers.

A The funeral service may take place at a crematorium

3 As the coffin is lowered into the ground, the minister scatters soil on it

Usually the family gathers after the funeral for something to eat or drink. In some communities the gathering becomes a celebration and thanksgiving for the life of the one who has died.

When the body is cremated the ashes are collected later. They are scattered in the garden of rest at the crematorium. Sometimes the person who has died leaves instructions about where the ashes should be scattered.

God's love is stronger than death

The funeral service varies from one church to another. For example, in the Roman Catholic Church there is a Mass at the start of the funeral. In all the Christian funeral services the message is the same – that the promise of God's love is stronger than death itself.

THINGS TO DO

1 Write the answers to these questions in full sentences. Who takes care of the arrangements for a Christian funeral? Where does the funeral take place?

2 Look at the photos and write a sentence or two about what the minister/priest is doing/saying in each picture.

3 A funeral may be a time to give thanks as well as a time to be sad. Design a symbol for a funeral service sheet which shows both of these ideas.

4 Life is stronger than death. Give two arguments to support or challenge this belief.

New words

cremation   crematorium

32

Islam: free to choose

Muslims believe that **Allah** is the giver of all life. This includes life after death. The Muslim holy book, the **Qur'an** (**A**) says:

> 'Surely He makes the dead alive and surely He has the power to do everything; there is no doubt that the hour will come and truly Allah will raise those who are in graves.'
>
> (22:5-7)

With the gift of life comes the freedom to choose how to live. A person can follow their own desires and live a selfish life. Or they can follow the will of Allah. Islam means 'submission' and Muslims are men and women who submit to the will of Allah.

B The world of work is not separate from the world of faith

A Muslims live by the teachings of the Qur'an

Discussion question

When we are given a choice about something we are also given responsibility. What examples can you give to show that this is true?

Trust and obey

In the Hadith, the Prophet **Muhammad** says:

> 'Every new born child is by nature a Muslim. It is his parents who make him a Jew, or a Christian.'

In other words, a child naturally learns to trust and obey. These are the qualities of the true Muslim.

The Five Pillars

There is no special ceremony to become a Muslim. Anyone who obeys the will of Allah is a Muslim. Muslims declare their faith saying the words:

'There is no God but Allah and Muhammad is Allah's Messenger.'

This statement of faith is called the Shahadah. The Shahadah is the first of the Five Pillars of Islam. The Five Pillars are the duties for all Muslims.

The second pillar is **Salah**. This is prayer five times a day. The Muslim day is structured by prayer (**B**). All Muslims must give two-and-a-half per cent of their savings to the poor. This is **Zakah**, the third pillar. The fourth pillar is the fast each year during the month of **Ramadan**. The fifth pillar is **Hajj** or pilgrimage. Every Muslim must go on pilgrimage to **Makkah** at least once in a lifetime.

In these ways the day, the year and the life of a Muslim are given shape and meaning by acts of submission and devotion to Allah.

New words

Allah   Qur'an   Muhammad   Salah
Zakah   Ramadan   Hajj   Makkah

THINGS TO DO

1 Write out the five pillars of Islam in your own words.

2 Write two headings:
   • The Muslim view
   • The non religious person's view.
   List three things about the Muslim view of life under the first heading. Then write the non-religious view of life under the other heading.

3 The Muslim day is shaped by prayer. How is your day shaped? Draw a diagram to show the shape of your day. Write a sentence about it.

4 Muslims believe that we are responsible for our actions. We will have to answer to Allah for what we have done. Write a story about someone who realizes for the first time that they are responsible for what they do.

C How is your day shaped?

33

Birth and naming

For Muslims, the birth of a baby is a time of great joy and thanksgiving. Muslim parents feel that it is a great responsibility and privilege to bring children into the world and to raise them in the Muslim faith.

Soon after the birth of a child, the father repeats the **Adhan** in the baby's right ear (**A**). This is the Muslim call to prayer. The **mu'adhin** says this five times a day from the **minaret** at the **mosque** (**B**). It begins with the words:

'*God is greatest' or 'Allahu Akbar'.*

This is repeated four times. Then the **Iqamah** (the call to the faithful) is whispered into the left ear of the baby.

B The call to prayer is heard five times a day

It ends with the words:

'*There is no God but Allah.'*

Purification

Several days after the birth of a child a ceremony is held at home. This is called the **aqiqah**. The baby's head is shaved as a symbol of **purification** (**C**). Parents give the weight of the hair in silver to charity.

The occasion is marked by a sacrifice. Two sheep are bought and killed if it is a boy and one if it is a girl. The meat is prepared

A The adhan is whispered in the baby's right ear

by the **halal** butcher and divided into three portions. One is kept for the family. Another is prepared for the friends and relatives as a meal. The third portion is given to the poor. In this way the family share their good fortune with others.

The naming of the child takes place on this occasion. For a baby boy it may be the name of one of the prophets in the Qur'an. A girl may also have a name taken from a woman in the scriptures.

Circumcision

Muslim boys are circumcised. Most Muslim parents arrange for it to happen at the hospital. It is often celebrated with a family gathering.

New words

Adhan	mu'adhin	minaret	mosque
Iqamah	aqiqah	purification	halal

---

1 Write out the statements which are true:
 • For Muslims, the birth of a child is something to celebrate.
 • Muslims take a new baby for granted.
 • Muslims feel it is a privilege to bring a child into the world.
 • Muslims feel a sense of responsibility to bring a child up in the Muslim faith.

2 Write down the following headings. Under each write about how the birth of a Muslim child is celebrated:
 • The Adhan and the Iqamah
 • The aqiqah
 • Naming the child.

3 'It is better to bring up a child in a religious faith than with no faith at all.' Write three arguments for or against this claim.

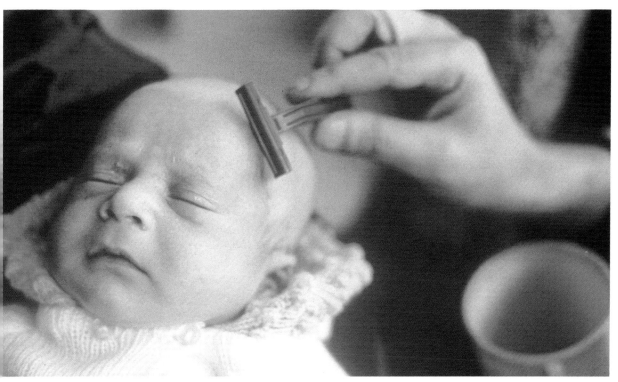

C The baby's hair is shaved as a sign of purification

34 Growing up in Islam

There is no special ceremony for becoming a Muslim. There is no rite of passage on becoming an adult. Muslim children go to classes at the Mosque to learn to read Arabic and to recite the Qur'an. The mosque school is called **madrasah** (A). Young Muslims learn about their faith. They begin to take responsibility for their religious life as they grow up. But that does not make them more Muslim than before.

Education

Education is very important in Islam. Young people are encouraged to spend a lot of time studying (B). Every young person learns to recite the Qur'an.

A Muslim children go to classes at the mosque

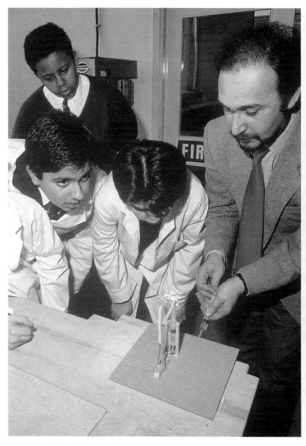

B Education is very important

Some choose to become **hafiz**. That is someone who can recite the Qur'an from memory (C).

Separate schools?

Most Muslim parents would like girls and boys to have separate classes in secondary school. This follows the teachings of the Qur'an. It says that women should avoid a situation where they are in male company without a member of the family there. It is believed that separate classes make it easier for young people to concentrate on their studies.

Many Muslim parents want their children to go to Muslim schools. This is so that the teaching of the faith can be central to their education.

Discussion question

In the UK there are **Roman Catholic** and **Church of England** state schools. Do you think that Muslims should have their own schools too?

New responsibilities

As they grow up, young Muslims are encouraged to become more responsible for following the teachings of the Qur'an. For example, men and women should dress modestly. For women this means wearing clothes that cover the body except for the face and hands.

Fasting during Ramadan is another important step in the life of the young Muslim. When a Muslim keeps the full fast for the first time there is a great sense of achievement. It shows a commitment to following the path of Islam.

THINGS TO DO

1 Write answers to the following questions in full sentences. How do Muslims mark the change from childhood to adulthood? What classes do young Muslims go to? Describe two new responsibilities a young Muslim takes on as s/he grows up.

2 Describe the things that you try to achieve in life as you grow up.

3 Think of two arguments you think a Muslim parent would give for separate classes for girls and boys. Say whether you agree with any of these arguments.

4 Design a poster which tells people about what it means to be a Muslim in the UK today.

New words

madrasah   hafiz   Roman Catholic Church of England

C Some young Muslims choose to learn the Qur'an by heart

35

Preparing for marriage

The Qur'an says that marriage was made to bring peace, love and protection for men and women. The Prophet Muhammad told his followers that marriage is a religious duty:

> 'When a worshipper of God has taken a wife he has perfected half of his religion.'
> **(Hadith)**

Muslim parents believe it is their duty to find a suitable partner for their son or daughter. Finding a partner is too important to be left to chance meetings (**A**).

Young muslims are advised against becoming too friendly with members of the opposite sex until they are ready for marriage. Islamic law forbids sexual relationships outside marriage.

B The interests and education of the young person are important

Assisted marriage

Because Muslim parents help to choose a marriage partner for their children, it has been called 'arranged marriage'. Many Muslims prefer to call it '**assisted marriage**'.

The parents introduce their son or daughter to a suitable partner. However, the young person has the right to say no. Muhammad said:

> 'A girl is to be asked whether she consents to marriage.'
> (Hadith)

A Finding a partner is too important to be left to chance meetings

---

Discussion question

What do you think Muslims look for in choosing a partner for their child?

Most young Muslims trust their parents to find someone who will make a good husband or wife. They look for someone with a similar commitment to Islam. They will also think about the interests and character of their son or daughter (**B**). Meetings between the families are arranged so that the couple can see each other. If they are both interested then they have a meeting where they can talk. Usually love comes after the marriage rather than before.

Family life

The Qur'an encourages Muslims to marry and have children. Happy family life leads to a happy society. A marriage is an important event for the whole community.

Islamic law allows a man to have up to four wives. However, the husband must be fair and treat them equally. Today, most Muslim men have only one wife (**C**).

C Most Muslim men now have only one wife

THINGS TO DO

1 Write out the sentences which are true:
   • The Prophet Muhammad said that marriage was a religious duty.
   • Muslims find a marriage partner through chance meetings.
   • Muslim parents believe it is their duty to find a marriage partner for their child.
   • The girl cannot refuse a partner.
   • The teachings of Islam say that the parents must get the consent of the child and not force a young person into marriage.

2 What will Muslim parents be looking for in choosing a partner for their son or daughter? Write your answer as an article for a Muslim newspaper.

3 What are the advantages and disadvantages of the parents assisting in finding a marriage partner? Write your answers in two columns. Do the same for finding your own marriage partner.

4 Happy family life makes a happy society. Show this in words and pictures.

New words

Hadith   assisted marriage

36

A Muslim wedding

In Islam, marriage is a human contract. It is also an agreement made before God. The families have been involved in assisting the marriage. They must therefore take some responsibility for making it work.

The wedding is an important event for the two families. Once the couple has agreed to marry a day is set. The two families decide on a dowry. This is a gift of money to the bride. It is called **mahr**. It is given by the groom. It remains the wife's property. Some of the mahr may be kept apart. This is for the wife in case of a divorce.

The ceremony

The marriage ceremony is sometimes held at the bride's family home or in a room at the local mosque (**A**). Friends and family come. The ceremony can be carried out by any Muslim male adult. It is usually the **imam**.

B Marriage customs vary

The groom, his father and the other male relatives gather in a room. The imam asks the groom if he consents to the marriage. Once he has consented the groom makes his marriage vows. The bride does not have to be there. Her father can represent her. She may be in a separate room with female members of the family. Witnesses tell her when the groom has made his solemn promise:

'I (name) take (name) as my lawfully wedded wife before Allah and in the presence of these witnesses, in accordance with the teachings of the holy Qur'an'.

Discussion question

Why is it important to have witnesses at a wedding?

Allah as witness

Allah is called upon as supreme witness to the vows. The groom promises that in his marriage he will serve Allah. It will therefore be a relationship of love, mercy and peace. The imam says prayers and verses from the Qur'an. After the groom has made his promises the bride makes her vows too. The bride and groom then sign copies of the marriage contract.

A A Muslim bride and groom on their wedding day

They keep one each.

At many Muslim weddings there are non-religious customs. These follow the formal ceremony. These vary from one community to another (**B**). One common tradition is the shared celebration meal (**C**).

THINGS TO DO

1 Design a wedding invitation for a Muslim wedding in the UK. Say where the wedding will be held. Say who will take the ceremony. Give names, dates and times.

2 Write an account of what happens at a Muslim wedding. Say what vows are made at the wedding ceremony.

3 Mahr is to give the wife security. What will make a person feel secure in a marriage relationship? Write your answer as an advice column for a Muslim magazine.

4 Do young people who are not religious need help and advice to make marriage work? Discuss this question in class.

> ## New words
>
> mahr   imam

C The shared meal after the wedding is celebrated in most communities

37 Life after death

Every day the Muslim says this prayer from the Qur'an (**A**):

'All praise is for Allah, the Lord of the Universe, the most merciful, the most kind; Master of the Day of Judgement. You alone we worship, from You alone we seek help. Guide us along the straight path.'

(Qur'an 1:1-7)

Every day Muslims remember that what they do in this life will decide what happens to them after death.

However, a Muslim should not serve Allah just for the sake of future rewards. A **Sufi** poet wrote:

*'O my Lord, if I worship You from fear of Hell, burn me in Hell, and if I worship You from hope of **Paradise**, exclude me there, but if I worship You for Your own sake then withhold not from me your Eternal Beauty.'*

New words

Sufi   Paradise   Day of Judgement
Akhira

Discussion question

What do you think the poet is saying in this poem?

Day of Judgement

The Qur'an says that there will be a **Day of Judgement.** Muslims believe that on this day everyone will be judged on the life

A Every day Muslims pray 'All praise is for Allah, the Lord of the Universe...'

they have led. Those who have followed the will of Allah will go to Paradise. Those who have ignored the will of Allah will be punished.

Muslims believe that after death, everyone will have to answer for what they have done. They say there are two angels watching over us. They keep a record of our actions.

Paradise and Hell

In the Qur'an, Paradise is described as a beautiful garden (**B**). Rivers flow there. There is no suffering, only perfect peace. In contrast, Hell is a place of torment.

Life after death

Life after death, **Akhirah**, is one of the basic beliefs of Islam. Every day Muslims remember that Allah is kind and merciful. Muslims believe Allah forgives those who are sorry and try to follow the straight path of islam.

THINGS TO DO

1 Write your answers to these questions. What does the daily prayer from the Qur'an say about Allah? Why should people worship Allah – what does the poet say?

2 Why does what we do in this life matter? Write your answer as a conversaton between a Muslim parent and child.

3 Design a poster showing the differences between Paradise and Hell.

B Paradise is described as being like a beautiful garden

38

Funeral rites

Muslims believe that this life is a preparation for life after death. They try to live a life guided by the Five Pillars. The last of these is Hajj. This is the pilgrimage to Makkah. It is seen by some as preparation for death (**A**). The sense of peace felt by pilgrims on Hajj is like the peace of Paradise. Hajj helps purify the soul of evil.

As Muslims near death, they say the Shahadah (see Unit 32). Friends and relatives read verses from the Qur'an with them. When death comes the family gathers to say these words from the Qur'an:

'We belong to Allah and to Him we shall return.'

Burial not cremation

In Islam the body is buried as soon as possible after death. Muslims believe that everyone will be raised from the dead. The body is not to be destroyed by **cremation**. It should be treated with great respect. It is washed three times as if for prayer. Then it is washed all over with soap and water. It is anointed and wrapped in three pieces of white cloth. If the dead person went on Hajj, these will be the cloths worn on the pilgrimage. The body is then laid on its left side in a coffin.

Discussion question

Most large mosques have a **mortuary**. Why do you think that this is?

The coffin is carried to the mosque. It is placed so that the body faces Makkah. Family and friends gather. The imam leads the prayers. The first chapter of the Qur'an is repeated.

A Many Muslims see the Hajj as a preparation for death

B The coffin is taken to the cemetery for burial

The coffin is taken to the cemetry for burial (**B**). As it is lowered into the grave, the words from the Qur'an are said:

'From the earth we did create you and into it you shall return and from it shall we bring you out once again.'

Night of Forgiveness

Muslims believe that it is important to pray for those who have died, especially for parents. In some places they have a night called the **Night of Forgiveness**. It is held during the fast of Ramadan. Muslims spend time in prayer. The men visit the graves of loved ones (**C**). They think about the Day of Judgment .

New words
cremation   mortuary Night of Forgiveness

THINGS TO DO

1 Answer the following questions in sentences.What words do Muslims recite when someone dies? Is the body cremated or buried? How is the body prepared for burial? Who leads prayers at the mosque? What what happens at the burial?

2 Write out the Five Pillars of Islam (see Unit 32). Say how one of these pillars can be a preparation for death.

3 Some people avoid thinking about their death and their funeral. Write a short conversation between someone like this and a Muslim who has thought about these things.

4 Remembering is one way to come to terms with the death of a loved one. Write a poem called 'Remembering'.

C Some Muslims visit the graves of loved ones

39

Sikhism: many lives, one journey

Sikhs believe that the soul travels through many lives. After many births in different bodies it becomes human. Only at this stage in the soul's journey can it attain **mukti**. This is when the soul is freed from the cycle of rebirth and finds union with God.

Discussion question

What does it mean to be 'free'? Are there different kinds of freedom?

God's grace

Being human offers the soul the opportunity to come close to God. Sikhs call God **Waheguru** meaning 'Wonderful Lord'. They believe that God awakens the human soul and calls men and women to him. It is by God's grace that the soul finds union (togetherness) with him.

The Sadhsangat

The Sikh community is called the **Sadhsangat**. This community helps Sikhs to grow morally and spiritually (**A**). The Sadhsangat is a model for society. Humility, tolerance, patience, service, justice, mercy and kindness are encouraged.

The Gurdwara

The **Gurdwara** is the Sikh place of worship. Here, the Sadhsangat puts these values into practice. The Gurdwara provides spiritual 'food' through the prayers and hymns (**kirtan**) and the reading of the scriptures (**B**).

The **langar** provides physical food and is an example of sharing (**C**). Sikhs believe that we must not waste the opportunity to grow in goodness and come close to God.

New words		
mukti	Waheguru	Sadhsangat
Gurdwara	kirtan	langar

A Where do children learn moral and spiritual values?

B The reading of the scriptures in the Gurdwara is spiritual food

C Shared food feeds the hungry and encourages kindness

THINGS TO DO

1 Write out the sentences that are true for Sikhs:
  - The soul lives through many lives.
  - Only when the soul becomes human can it reach mukti.
  - Sikhs believe there is no God.
  - Mukti is freedom from the cycle of rebirth.
  - The soul does not need God.
  - God awakens the soul and calls men and women to union with him.

2 Draw a diagram showing both physical needs (for example food) and moral or spiritual 'food' that a person needs.

3 What are the opportunities human life offers? Write your answer in a letter to a Sikh friend who has explained his/her beliefs about life.

4 Schools are required by law to provide for moral and spiritual development of the pupils. Can schools help young people to grow morally and spiritually? How should a school try to do this? Discuss your ideas and write them for a classroom display.

40

All stages in life are one

Guru Nanak (**A**) was the first Sikh Guru. He said that the way to God is open to every human being. It does not matter which religion or social class they belong to. He said that God must be found in everyday life.

Guru Nanak said that all people can get close to God. Some people believed that you could only get close to God if you gave up home and family to live in the forest (**B**). They believed that you had to live a very hard life, practising difficult forms of **yoga,** meditating and begging for food. Guru Nanak said there is no need to shut yourself off from the world in this way. God can be found in everyday life.

No stages in life

Others believed that you could only reach freedom in the final stage of life. They said you had to first be a student, then a householder earning a living and raising a family.

Only after retirement could a person try to get close God. Guru Nanak rejected this idea. He said that the way to mukti is open to everyone. It did not matter what their age or their stage in life.

Discussion question

Do you think that there are times when people naturally turn to God? When is this and why is this?

A Guru Nanak, the first Sikh Guru

B You do not have to do difficult yoga to find God

The world of work

Sikhs believe we are all a part of the world of work (**C**). We all have responsibilities. We all have a role to play in the community. No one can survive without other people. It is therefore right that everyone takes part. Everyone should earn a living by honest means and share their resources.

Guru Nanak said men and women must remember God at all times. When they are at work or involved in home and family they should still remember God. There is no need to wait until these things are out of the way. In a community that serves the needs of everyone there is an opportunity to come to know and love God.

1 Write down the sentences which show Sikh beliefs:
- The way to God is open to everyone.
- You have to give up family life to get close to God.
- God can be found in the world of work and in everyday life.
- Earning a living is bad.
- There is no need to live apart from the world to find God.
- Everyone can become close to God, no matter what their age or stage in life.

2 Design a poster to show the Sikh belief that the way to God is open to everyone.

3 If we rely on the world of work, should we contribute to it? Discuss your ideas and write down the different points of view in the debate.

4 Many people do not stop to think about where life is leading. Write a poem or a diary entry in which a person thinks about this question.

New words

Guru Nanak   yoga

C We are all a part of the world of work

41 The naming ceremony

Sikhs believe that this life is a precious gift. Birth is a time of joy and giving thanks to God. In the **Guru Granth Sahib**, the Sikh holy scriptures, it says:

> 'Joy abounds in all creation, praise Him you who love your Lord God Almighty.......God is gracious, filled with mercy, Nanak thus proclaims this truth.'

When a baby is born, prayers of thanks like this are said from the Guru Granth Sahib. Sometimes a prayer is whispered in the ear of the newborn child. In some cases, the whole Guru Granth Sahib is read to mark the event.

Thanksgiving

The parents take gifts to the Gurdwara as a sign of their thanks. They may give a **rumala**. This is a silk cloth to cover the Guru Granth Sahib.

At a later date they may arrange the community meal in the langar. There they can share their happiness with others.

Discussion question

Sharing happiness is important. Why do we need to share our joys and successes?

Later a naming ceremony is held at the Gurdwara (A). The **granthi** leads the ceremony (**B**). He carefully lifts the pages of the holy book and lets them fall open. The first letter for the child's name is

A The joy of the birth is shared with the community at the naming ceremony

B The granthi reading from the scriptures

taken from the first letter of the first word at the start of the hymn on the the left hand page. The parents choose a name and the granthi says a blessing.

Amrit

Sometimes the child is given **amrit** . This is a mixture of sugar and water. It is stirred with a double-edged sword called a **khanda**. Prayers are said over it. The granthi dips the khanda into the amrit. He lightly touches the tongue of the baby.

Sikh first names are chosen for their meaning. Most of the names can be for a boy or a girl. **Guru Gobind Singh** wanted all Sikhs to be equal. He said that the second name should be **Kaur** meaning 'Princess' for a girl. It should be **Singh** meaning 'Lion' for a boy.

New words

Guru Granth Sahib   rumala   granthi
amrit   khanda   Guru Gobind Singh
Kaur   Singh

THINGS TO DO

1 Answer the following questions in full sentences:
   - What happens when a baby is born into a Sikh family?
   - How do the parents show their thanks to God?
   - When is the naming ceremony?
   - How is the name chosen?
   - What is amrit?
   - What is special about Sikh names?

2 Design an invitation to a Sikh naming ceremony. Use symbols from the ceremony. Invite everyone to the langar or community meal after the ceremony.

3 Sharing happiness with others is important. Write a story or play in which a person shares their happiness with the community around them.

4 Sikh names have meanings. For example Gurbakhsh Singh means 'Blessed by the Guru.' What names would you choose for your children and why? Choose three different names.

42

Taking Amrit

As they grow up, young Sikhs take part in a ceremony called **amrit chakna**. This is an **initiation** ceremony. It is when they become members of the **Khalsa**, the community of committed Sikhs.

The ceremony was introduced by Guru Gobind Singh, at the festival of **Baisakhi** in 1699. Five men were willing to give up their lives for the Sikh faith. He called them the **Panj Piare,** the Five Pure Ones (**A**). They were the first members of the Khalsa.

Discussion question

Why do you think that Guru Gobind Singh called the five men the Five Pure Ones?

Making promises

The amrit ceremony is held at the Gurdwara. Those taking amrit bathe and put on clean clothes. Five members of the Khalsa, called the Panj Piare, perform the ceremony. Those taking amrit promise to follow the teachings of the Gurus. They also promise:

- To pray daily: before dawn, after sunset and before bed

- To wear the **Five Ks**, the symbols of the Sikh faith: **Kesh**, long hair; **Kangha**, comb; **Kara**, bracelet; **Kachera**, shorts; and **Kirpan**, sword

- To avoid all intoxicating drinks and drugs

- To be faithful in marriage.

Hymns are sung from the Guru Granth Sahib. The Panj Piare prepare a bowl of amrit or nectar. They stir the mixture with the khanda (**B**). Prayers are said over it. Those who are taking amrit kneel. The nectar is given five times into their cupped hands. It is sprinkled over their eyes and on their head five times. They declare:

*'The khalsa is dedicated to God.
The victory belongs to God alone.'*

All who receive amrit drink the remaining nectar. At the end they say the **Mool Mantar** five times.

A Guru Gobind Singh and the Panj Piare

B Preparing amrit

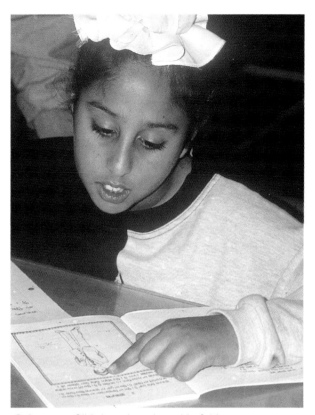

C A young Sikh learning about his faith

After the ceremony

After the ceremony, boys receive the name Singh and girls the name Kaur. These replace the family name. This is to break down barriers as names were used to show a person's social class. At the end of the ceremony a prayer called the **Ardas** is recited. Everyone then receives **karah parshad** (blessed food).

Sikhs can become members of the Khalsa at any age. They must understand the promises they are making (**C**). Many take amrit just as they become adults.

THINGS TO DO

1 Complete the following sentences:
The Sikh initiation ceremony is called....
The ceremony was introduced by.....
The Panj Piare were the first members of the .....
Panj Piare means...........

2 Prepare an invitation to the amrit ceremony. Say what happens at the ceremony.

3 Describe the kind of ceremony you think would suit a non-religious person approaching adulthood.

4 Sikhs have a strong sense of identity and responsibility. Write down three things that can help give young people today a sense of identity and responsibility.

New words

amrit chakna   initiation   Khalsa
Baisakhi   Panj Piare   Five Ks
Kesh   Kangha   Kara   Kachera
Kirpan   Mool Mantar Ardas
karah parshad

43

Marriage

Sikhs believe that marriage is the union of two people in body, mind and soul. It is a relationship for life. It is built on respect, love, equality and faithfulness (**A**).

Sikhs consider it their duty to find a marriage partner for their son or daughter. The young person is involved in the decision. If they do not accept the parents' choice, the search for another partner begins.

Ceremony of bliss

The Sikh wedding is called the **anand karaj**. This means 'the ceremony of bliss'. It must take place in the presence of the Guru Granth Sahib. Most marriages are held at the Gurdwara (**B**). The two families greet each other and they exchange gifts.

The religious service begins with the musicians playing hymns. The bride and groom sit facing the Guru Granth Sahib. The granthi usually conducts the service.

The Lavan

The couple is asked whether they wish to marry. They accept by bowing before the Guru Granth Sahib. The bride's father takes one end of the groom's scarf and puts it in the hand of his daughter. The marriage hymn from the Guru Granth Sahib is read. This is the **Lavan**. It is a hymn of praise to God. It celebrates the love of the marriage relationship. The love and closeness between husband and wife is a model for the love and closeness that can be between the soul and God.

The couple walk four times around the Guru Granth Sahib. The first time is for a life of sharing in work. The second is for coming together in love without fear. The third is for not caring about possessions. The last is for the peace of perfect union.

A Sikh marriage is based on respect, humility and equality

B Most Sikh marriages take place at the Gurdwara

Discussion question

Why does the couple walk around the Guru Granth Sahib? What might it show?

The couple is declared husband and wife. They are showered with flower petals. The granthi opens the Guru Granth Sahib. He takes the reading from where the pages fall open. This is the final prayer. Everyone receives karah parshad. There is a festive meal and celebration.

New words

anand karaj   Lavan

THINGS TO DO

1 Answer the following questions in sentences:
   • What is the Sikh wedding called?
   • Where is it held?
   • What happens at the service?
   • What is the Lavan?

2 Draw and explain the meaning of the joining with the scarf and the walking around the scriptures.

3 Do you think that marriage is a time for learning? What lessons can people learn through being married?

4 'Love without fear' How can a couple make sure that fear does not creep into their marriage relationship? Write your answer as an advice column for a magazine.

44

Death and cremation

Sikhs believe that it is possible to reach perfect peace and freedom (mukti) in this life. A Sikh can reach mukti by following the teachings of the Gurus and meditating on the name of God (see Unit 39). If a person reaches mukti, they are united with God when they die. If the soul does not reach mukti it will be born again in another body. It then continues its journey.

When a Sikh dies the family says prayers from the Guru Granth Sahib. The body is washed with a mixture made from water and yoghurt. Clean clothes are put on. If the person was a Khalsa Sikh, the body is dressed in the Five Ks.

Cremation

In India the **cremation** takes place outside. In the UK Sikhs use the local crematorium (**A**). In some communities, the coffin is first taken to the Gurdwara. It is placed before the Guru Granth Sahib. Friends and relatives can pay their respects there (**B**).

On the day of the cremation, prayers are said for the soul of the dead person. The coffin is then taken to the crematorium. Close family members and friends follow. The granthi says the **Kirtan Sohila**. This is the evening prayer.

> 'Know the real purpose of being here and gather up your treasure under the guidance of the True Guru. Make your mind God's home. If he lives within you undisturbed, you will not be reborn.'

The coffin is then taken away for cremation.

Discussion question

Sometimes Sikhs have to use a chapel with Christian symbols at the crematorium. What should crematoriums do to serve people of different faiths?

A In the UK cremation takes place in the local crematorium

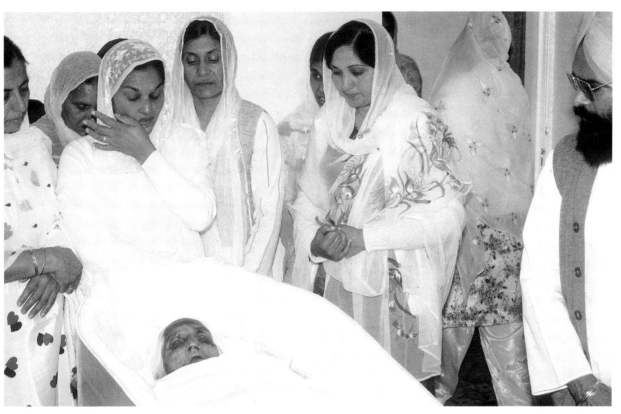

B People can pay their respects at the Gurdwara

After the cremation there is a service at the Gurdwara. Friends say a few words to express their love and respect for the one who has died. The service ends with the usual prayer called the Ardas. Karah parshad is shared out.

Scattering the ashes

After a few days the ashes are collected from the crematorium. They are scattered on the waters of a river. The family usually arranges a complete reading of the Guru Granth Sahib at the Gurdwara. Towards the end of the reading friends and relatives gather again to comfort the family.

New words

cremation   crematorium   Kirtan Sohila

1 Answer the following questions. Do Sikhs bury or cremate their dead? How is the body prepared? Where does the coffin stay before the cremation - why? What happens on the day of the cremation? What prayer is said on this occasion?

2 The soul may be united with God or may return to live again. Draw a diagram using words and pictures to show and explain these Sikh beliefs.

3 'Know the real purpose of being here.' What do you think is the real purpose of being here? Write your response as a diary entry.

4 Kirtan Sohila (evening prayer) suggests that death is the night before the new day. Design a card for those in mourning using this idea. Write your own poem inside.

45

Shared concerns

The student of religion cannot agree with someone who says that all religions are the same.

They are not. There are important differences in practice and belief.

The religions have different beliefs and practices. Yet they do have share concerns. For example, they all make us ask the question: 'Where am I going?'

Not one of the great world religions says to its followers: 'You can go your own way. Do your own thing. Forget about anyone else. Just do what you want – it does not really matter.'

All the religions say it does matter how we live our lives.

Milestones of life

Religious ceremonies mark the important milestones of life. All offer the opportunity for the people present to think about their own spiritual journey (**C**).

At the Anglican christening everyone is asked to promise to serve Christ. At the Jewish wedding, a glass is broken to remind people that this is a serious occasion as well as a joyful one. At a Sikh funeral, everyone is asked to 'Know the real purpose of being here.'

A Orthodox churches have icons of the saints who have lived in the past

B Buddhists meditate on the way all things pass away

The great religious traditions do not allow a person to travel without any cares on their journey through life. There are decisions to make and responsibilities to take on. There are talents that must not be wasted. There are others who need our help – and sometimes we will need theirs.

Look for what lasts

In the Orthodox Church, the **icons** of the **saints** (**A**) remind Christians that many have lived before them. This life will pass away.

One of the meditations Buddhist monks have to do is to watch the process of decay (**B**). In this way they learn that nothing lasts.

The world's great religions all challenge men and women to look for the unchanging and everlasting.

New words

icons   saints

C All the major religions ask their followers to think about their direction in life!

Glossary

A

Adhan Muslim call to prayer

Akhirah everlasting life, life after death

Allah Muslim name for God

Altar table in church from where the Eucharist (bread and wine) is given

Amrit nectar made from sugar and water

Amrit chakna Sikh initiation ceremony

Anand karaj Sikh wedding ceremony, ceremony of bliss

Anglican Christian family of Churches which includes the Church of England

Anicca 'impermanence', belief that nothing lasts or has lasting reality

Anoint to put on oil or perfume as a part of a religious ceremony

Anointed marked with oil. This is often part of a ceremony to make someone king

Aqiqah ritual shaving of baby's head

Ardas formal prayer said in the Gurdwara, sometimes called the standing prayer as Sikhs always stand for it

Ashrama a stage of life (of which there are four in the Hindu tradition)

Assisted marriage marriage in which the parents help in finding a partner for son/daughter

Atman soul, self

B

Baisakhi Sikh festival celebrating the beginning of Sikh Khalsa

Baptism rite of initiation which involves sprinkling with water or immersion in water

Baptist Christian belonging to Baptist Church, a Protestant Church which rejects practice of infant baptism

Baptistry pool or area in church used for Believer's Baptism

Bar Mitzvah when a Jewish boy becomes a Son of the Commandment at the age of 13, a ceremony to mark a Jewish boy's coming of age

Bat Mitzvah when a Jewish girl becomes a Daughter of the Commandment, a ceremony to mark a Jewish girl's coming of age

Believer's Baptism ritual immersion in water as a sign of commitment to Christ

Bible Christian holy scriptures containing the Old and New Testament; name used for the Jewish Tenakh (which Christians call the Old Testament)

Bimah platform from where the holy Torah is read in the synagogue

Bishop senior member of the Church priesthood in Anglican, Roman Catholic and Orthodox Churches

Bodhisattva one who delays Buddhahood in order to help others

Brahmin priest, member of the priestly class in traditional Hindu caste system

Breaking of Bread see Eucharist

Brit Milah rite of circumcision

C

Christening infant baptism

Church of England the established Church of England

Circumcision when the foreskin of the penis has been surgically removed

Confession when someone accepts responsibility for their wrong doings

Confirmed when a believer makes firm their faith with promises

Consecrates makes holy

Covenant sacred agreement between God and his people

Cremation burning of a corpse to reduce it to ashes

Crematorium place where cremations take place

D

Day of Judgement religious belief in a day at the end of time when all people will be judged according to their deeds

Dedication service of thanksgiving for birth of a child

Devil the power of evil sometimes described as a person

Dhamma teachings of the Buddha

Dharma duty, law, religion, religious duty

Dukkha suffering, imperfection

E

Eightfold Path eight teachings of the Buddha on how to live

Enlightenment understanding the truth

F

Eucharist thanksgiving service in which Christians remember the last supper Jesus shared with his disciples, also called Holy Communion, Mass, Breaking of Bread, The Lord's Supper

First Communion special service to mark the first time a Roman Catholic receives the host in the service of the Mass or Eucharist

Five Ks five symbols worn by Sikhs – all beginning with the letter K

Font bowl or container for the water used for infant baptism

Four Noble Truths the first teachings of the Buddha

G

Gayatri mantra daily prayer for enlightenment recited by Hindus

Genesis first book of the Jewish Torah and the Christian Bible

Ghee clarified butter used in Hindu worship

Granthi one who leads the worship in the Gurdwara

Gurdwara Sikh place of worship

Guru spiritual teacher, religious teacher

Guru Gobind Singh tenth Sikh Guru

Guru Granth Sahib Sikh holy scriptures

Guru Nanak the first of the Ten Gurus of Sikhism

H

Hadith the sayings of the Prophet Muhammad

Hafiz one who can recite the Qur'an from memory

Hajj pilgrimage to Makkah

Halal fit, lawful, permitted

Havan fire ritual used in Hindu worship

Heaven place of existence after death when the good and faithful will live in the presence of God

Hell place or existence after death when those who have lived evil lives and who have rejected God's forgiveness will be separated from God

Holy Communion see Eucharist

Holy Spirit the power and presence of God working in the lives of Christians

Host wafer representing bread from the last supper

Huppah canopy used in Jewish wedding under which the couple stand

I

Icons image, painting or mosaic of saint used in devotion in the Orthodox Church

Infant baptism Christian rite in which a baby is anointed with consecrated water and welcomed into the church in Anglican, Orthodox and Roman Catholic traditions

Initiation ceremony to mark a new stage in life

Iqamah call to stand for prayer in Islam

K

Kachera shorts worn by Sikhs. One of the Five Ks

Kaddish prayer recited by mourners

Kamma action, intentional action

Kangha comb worn in the hair by Sikhs. One of the Five Ks

Kara steel bracelet worn by Sikhs. One of the Five Ks

Karah parshad blessed food shared out at Sikh worship

Karma actions, the effects and results of actions

Kaur 'princess', name given to Sikh girls at the amrit ceremony

Kesh long, uncut hair. One of the Five Ks

Ketubah Jewish marriage contract

Khalsa community of committed Sikhs

Khanda double edged ceremonial sword

Kirpan sword, symbol of the sword worn by Sikhs. One of the Five Ks

Kirtan Sikh devotional song or hymn

Kirtan Sohila Sikh evening prayer

Kosher foods permitted by Jewish dietary law

Kshatriya warrior or ruling class in traditional Hindu caste system

L

Langar shared meal, community kitchen at the Gurdwara

Lavan Sikh marriage ceremony

Lay community community of men and women who are not ordained as priests, monks or nuns

Lord's Supper see Eucharist

M

Madrasah Qur'an school

Mahayana "great way". a main form of Buddhism in which belief in bodhisattras is important

Mahr wedding dowry paid by the bridegroom

Makkah holy city for Muslims, birthplace of the Prophet Muhammad

Mass see Eucharist

Meditation practice of calming and disciplining the mind

Messianic Age Jewish belief in a time when God's reign will be established on Earth

Milestones important point in the journey of life

Minaret tall tower from which the call to prayer is given

Minister one who leads the worship in a church

Minyan ten adult male Jews, minimum number required for worship in many synagogues

Mohel trained surgeon who performs rite of circumcision

Moksha liberation from cycle of karma and samsara, union with God

Mool Mantar Sikh statement of faith or prayer about God summed up in the words of Guru Nanak

Mortuary place where the body is prepared for burial

Mosque place of prostration, place of prayer

Mu'adhin one who calls the faithful to prayer from the minaret at the mosque

Muhammad name of the last of God's messengers and prophets according to the Qur'an. Whenever Muslims mention his name they add the words 'peace be upon him'. When written this is sometimes shortened to 'pbuh'

Mukti liberation from endless cycle of rebirth and blissful union with God

N

Nibbana 'blowing out', a state of perfect peace

Night of Forgiveness a special night of prayer and fasting when Muslims remember the Day of Judgement

O

Ordination rite marking the beginning of a religious way of life, usually involving promises

Orthodox Churches family of Churches including Greek, Russian and Eastern European Churches. Not Roman Catholic or Protestant Churches

P

Pali language that buddhist scriptures are written in

Panj piare the five pure ones, those initiated into the Khalsa

Paradise place of perfect peace and joy where the faithful are rewarded for their good deeds after death

Priest one who carries out religious rituals and leads worship

Prophets people sent by God to speak God's message

Protestant Churches branch of the church which rejected the authority of the Pope

Puja worship, usually involving offerings at a shrine

Purgatory place or existence after death where those who have repented their sin and accept God's forgiveness are purified in readiness for heaven

Purification symbolic or ritual cleansing/washing

Q

Qur'an the Muslim holy scriptures

R

Rabbi teacher, leader in the Jewish community

Ramadan the ninth month of the Islamic calendar, during which fasting is required

Ravana evil tyrant in the story of Rama

Registry Office local authority office where births, marriages and deaths are registered

Reform Jews affirm the importance of interpreting God's commandments in the light of contemporary religious debate

Repent to say or feel sorry with the intention of doing better in the future

Resurrection the rising from the dead of Jesus Christ

Rites of Passage religious rituals or ceremonies

River Ganges most sacred pilgrimage site for Hindus

Roman Catholic branch of Christian Church governed by the Pope

Rumala decorative silk cloth used to cover the Sikh Scriptures

S

Sacred Thread ceremony ritual at the Hindu boy's entrance to the first stage of life – the student stage

Sadhsangat the true community or assembly of Sikhs

Saints holy people now holding a special place in heaven

Salah Muslim set prayer said five times a day. One of the Five Pillars of Islam

Samskar rituals marking stages in life cycle

Sandek one who holds the baby at Brit Milah, godfather

Sangha community of ordained monks and nuns in Buddhism

Sannyasin one who is in the fourth stage of life in Hindu tradition, a wandering holy man

Shabbat the day of rest and renewal at the end of the week which starts at sunset on Friday and ends at nightfall on Saturday

Shivah seven days of intense mourning following the burial of a close relation

Singh 'lion', name given to Sikh males at the amrit ceremony

Sufi Muslim mystic, one who sees the oneness of God in all things

Sukkot a Jewish harvest festival, Jews build temporary booths to live in for this time

Synagogue place of congregation, Jewish place of worship

T

Tallit prayer shawl

Tefillin small leather boxes containing the words of the Torah worn by Jewish males during weekday prayers

Ten Precepts rules for living in the Sangha accepted at Buddhist ordination

Tenakh the law, the prophets and the writings, Jewish Bible

Theravada "way of the elders'. A main form of Buddhism developed in Sri Lanka and South East Asia

Three Jewels the three refuges, the Buddha, Dhamma and the Sangha

Tilak red mark on forehead worn in religious ceremonies and worn by Hindu brides

Torah the first five books of the Jewish bible, the most sacred of Jewish scripture

V

Vaishya the merchant and business class in traditional Hindu caste system

Vihara temple

Vishnu one of the main forms of God in Hinduism, who comes to earth in different forms

W

Waheguru Wonderful Lord, God

Y

Yarhzeit anniversary of death marked in Jewish community

Yoga self discipline in life, exercises to control mind and body

Z

Zakah giving to the poor and needy. One of the Five Pillars of Islam